How to be an
Even Better Chair

SOPHIE PETIT-ZEMAN

WITH A FOREWORD BY JULIA MIDDLETON

How to be an Even Better Chair

Sensible advice from the public and charity sectors

Harlow, England • London • New York • Boston • San Francisco • Toronto • Sydney • Tokyo • Singapore • Hong Kong
Seoul • Taipei • New Delhi • Cape Town • Madrid • Mexico City • Amsterdam • Munich • Paris • Milan

PEARSON EDUCATION LIMITED

Edinburgh Gate
Harlow CM20 2JE
Tel: +44 (0)1279 623623
Fax: +44 (0)1279 431059
Website: www.pearsoned.co.uk

First published in Great Britain in 2006

The right of Sophie Petit-Zeman to be identified as author of this work has been asserted by her in accordance with the Copyright and Designs and Patents Act 1988

ISBN-13: 978-0-273-70729-5
ISBN-10: 0-273-70729-9

British Library Cataloguing in Publication Data
A catalog record for this book is available from the British Library

Library of Congress Cataloging-in-Publication Data
Petit-Zeman, Sophie, 1965–
    How to be an even better chair : sensible advice about chairing in the charity, not-for-profit, and public sectors / Sophie Petit-Zeman.
       p. cm.
    ISBN–10: 0-273-70729–9
    ISBN–13: 978-0-273-70729–5 (pbk.)
       1. Charities--Management. 2. Nonprofit organizations--Management. 3. Associations, institutions, etc.--Management. 4. Boards of directors. I. Title.

    HV41.P457 2006
    658.4'22--dc22

10 9 8 7 6 5 4 3 2
10 09 08 07 06

Typeset in 9.5pt Iowan by 70
Printed and bound in Great Britain by Bell & Bain Ltd, Glasgow

The Publisher's policy is to use paper manufactured from sustainable forests.

Contents

About the author

Dr Sophie Petit-Zeman migrated from medical research to communications and journalism, focusing on science, medicine and social care. She sits on more committees than a person should, is a Trustee of the Brain and Spine Foundation and, after completing this book, was appointed Director of Public Dialogue at the Association of Medical Research Charities.

Foreword
By Julia Middleton, *Chief Executive, Common Purpose*

This book came about because many of us felt we were not chairing as well as we could or should.

Over the past couple of years, groups of senior leaders have been gathering at an event run by Common Purpose called OpenGround to talk about issues they feel passionate about and how they can support each other to make change happen. One of the big challenges they identified was how to improve the quality of chairing in the UK.

There is not enough diversity on boards, which can appear complacent and can cause opportunities and important angles to be missed. If more diverse boards are to succeed, they will demand better chairing. There is talent everywhere and we cannot afford to waste it just because someone does not look like a leader or act like all the others.

Those who met through OpenGround and who were concerned about the quality of chairing in the UK have been meeting over supper and exchanging wisdom and ideas for effective chairing. It's the ideas that came out of those conversations that form the basis of this book. My father always said, "Any fool can make things more complicated; it's the really talented people who make things simple." And that's what I watched and heard through working with the many able chairs involved in this book.

What's the simple message? The best chairs are people who know that they exist to make sure their organization is delivering to the people it has set out to serve. Not to support the chief executive (CEO), not to represent the organization, not to build partnerships with others, but to ensure they are delivering what it says "on the tin" to the people they serve. Things do seem to go wrong when chairs forget this.

The great chairs never forget the objective. They have a passion that is infectious, they don't duck the difficult questions or people and, perhaps most importantly, they are confident enough that they don't need to play status games with the CEO or other board members, with the staff, with the stakeholders or the swanks or the people who live in their housing or receive their care or learn in their institutions.

We all found existing models for chairing rather frustrating and unhelpful. And best-practice guides often don't match the situation. The reality is that chairing is an enormous act of balancing and sometimes it gets out of kilter. That is when you need a "real practice" guide from people who have done it, learned from it, made the mistakes and are still trying to get the balance right.

Stories and conversations helped a lot. So this book is not intended to be the definitive guide to chairing. You must not read it for the full story on chairing. You will need other books for the rules, the codes, the structures and the systems. This is the book to read after you have read the others and you want to tap into the experience of chairs who have learned the hard way about chairing. We hope it will act as a springboard for you to begin your own conversations with other chairs about how chairs can make positive change happen.

Don't let this real practice guide put you off. It can be pretty daunting when you see all the pitfalls laid out, when you hear the types of mistakes even experienced chairs make and think how easy it would be to fall into that trap. But don't be put off. Go back to the objective of the organization and remember why you are there as a chair: to deliver to the people the organization has been set up to serve. You hold a key to making sure people get decent healthcare, to challenging our schools to deliver the best education to our young people, to helping refugees to settle and belong. These are real things to achieve, important things that touch and change others' lives, and that is a glorious thing to do, however tough.

Leadership can be a lonely task. Hopefully as you read this short book, you will feel slightly less out on a limb and remember that there are lots of us struggling to get chairing right. And those of you who are not yet chairing may be better prepared when you do.

Join the conversation. Share your chairing experiences by emailing me at julia middleton@commonpurpose.org.uk *and help to make boards all across the UK stronger and more effective.*

Acknowledgements

Sophie would like to offer huge thanks to all those who talked to her about chairing, on and off the record, to her dream of an editor, Rachael Stock, and her favourite husband, Emmanuel Petit.

Julia would like to say thanks to Rachael Stock who, in addition to being a great publisher, is a lifelong campaigner and instantly recognized the impact better chairing could have on the UK. Thanks also to Peter Sherratt and Lehman Brothers for their support in making this book a reality.

Introducing the chairs

This book is essentially the collected wisdom of a group of experienced chairs, most of whom have been meeting regularly over a period of a year or more to share thoughts, experiences and insights. Throughout the book, ideas and observations are often attributed to individual chairs, and so here we give you a brief rundown of who they are and what they do.

Zenna Atkins is Chair of Portsmouth NHS Teaching Primary Care Trust, Places for People group (a national property management, regeneration, social care and house-building company), Dreamwall (an innovative young people's organization) and a non-executive Director within the Royal Navy. She is an executive consultant with Social Solutions and supports her family running a restaurant in Southsea. She is a former chief executive in the voluntary sector, senior local government officer and award-winning entrepreneur.

Carolyn Berkeley is Chair of the Enfield Primary Care Trust, a member of the NHS Confederation Council and a member of the Council on Tribunals. She has been a school governor and a board member of various voluntary organizations and is a Justice of the Peace.

Jane Campbell is an independent health and social care policy adviser. She was Chair of the Social Care Institute for Excellence (SCIE), which works to improve the quality of social care across England, Wales and Northern Ireland. Previously, she co-founded and directed the National Centre for Independent Living. Between 1991 and 1995, she was Chairperson of the British Council of Disabled People. Jane has been a Commissioner of the Disability Rights Commission since its formation in 2000.

Pamela Chesters is Chair of the Royal Free Hampstead NHS Trust and the Royal Free Hampstead Charitable Trust. She also chairs the English Churches Housing Group and is a former chair of Opera Della Luna. Prior to her chairing responsibilities, Pam was the Chief Executive of Duckhams Oils.

Graham Creelman is Chair of Screen East, the Regional Cultural Consortium and the East of England Development Agency's Creative Industries Sector, as well as Governor of the Norwich School of Art. He is also

Managing Director of Anglia Television and the Director of Regional Programming for ITV Broadcasting.

Andrew Cubie currently chairs Quality Scotland (an organization committed to business excellence), The Centre for Healthy Working Lives, Scotland's Garden Trust and the Royal National Lifeboat Institution. He is the former Chair of the Confederation of British Industry in Scotland. He was the Convenor of the Independent Committee of Inquiry into Student Finance in Scotland (the "Cubie Committee"), which brought about the abolition of tuition fees in Scotland. He holds a number of non-executive directorships in public, private and voluntary companies ranging from investment trusts to kilt manufacturers and including Common Purpose and the British Council. Andrew is a Consultant to the law firm Fyfe Ireland WS and has variously been Chairman and Senior Partner of that firm, specializing in corporate law.

Richard Ellis chairs the East of England Development Agency and is Chairman of Governors of the Earlham Early Years Centre. A Chartered Management Accountant, Richard is still active in business, running Norfolk Country Cottages, and is also a board member of the Theatre Royal, Norwich, the Forum Trust and HEART.

Stephen Falder, in addition to being Marketing Director of Manchester-based HMG Paints Ltd, is the Trust Chairman of Community Forests North West. He is an active voice for industry, being a Regional Councillor and member of the SME Council for the CBI. He is a past president of the British Coatings Foundation and is Chairman of the fully licensed Sector Skills Council Proskills.

Simon Fanshawe, writer and broadcaster, is Chair of the Brighton & Hove Economic Partnership, Made in Brighton Ltd (a theatre investment fund), Midnight Communications (a PR company), Brighton Festival Fringe Ltd and Brighton Festival and Dome Ltd. He has been an active member of several boards, both commercial and voluntary, including the gay and lesbian equality lobby Stonewall and the Edinburgh Festival Fringe.

Imtiaz Farookhi is Chief Executive of the National House-Building Council (NHBC) and Chairman of CNLIS, as well as serving on the boards of the Thames Gateway Urban Development Corporation and South East England Development Agency. He is also a non-executive director of the British Board of Agremont (BBA).

John Gardiner was Chief Executive and Chair of Laird Group plc, and Chairman of Tesco plc from 1997 to 2004, having previously been a non-executive director. He has been a non-executive director of a number of other corporations including British Airways, British Leyland, British Shipbuilders, Courtaulds, PowerGen and 3i Group. He has also served as a member of many boards including National Enterprise, the South Bank Theatre and the Council of Open University, and as Chairman of the Council of Brunel University, Brunel Science Park and the School Teachers' Review Body. In 1998, John was appointed to the board of *The Economist* newspaper.

Richard Greenhalgh is Chair of Templeton College Oxford, Care International UK, the Council for Industry and Higher Education, and First Milk, as well as serving as Vice Chair of the Qualifications and Curriculum Authority. He is a non-executive director of Rank Group Plc and an adviser to the Boards of Calor, UK and All Nippon Airways. He sits on the Council of the Royal Society of Arts. Richard was Chairman of Unilever UK until 2004, having worked for the company for over thirty years in the UK and abroad.

Michael Hastings is Chair of Crime Concern and was a founding trustee 15 years ago. He sits on the boards of Comic Relief, Children in Need, Fame Academy Bursary Fund and the World Service Trust. Michael is International Director for Corporate Citizenship for KPMG Worldwide, and was previously Head of Corporate Social Responsibility at the BBC as well as a Commissioner with the Commission for Racial Equality.

Deirdre Hutton was Chair of the Food Standards Agency and was Deputy Chair of the Financial Services Authority. She also chaired the Food Chain Centre and the National Consumer Council as well as serving on various other public bodies.

David Isaac is Chair of Stonewall and Modern Art Oxford, and a trustee of the Diana Princess of Wales fund. He is also a partner in the international law firm Pinsent Masons. He has previously served as a member of a number of boards in the public and private sectors.

Bill Kilgallon is Chief Executive of the Social Care Institute for Excellence. He chaired the Leeds Teaching Hospitals NHS Trust from 1998 to 2003 and has been a board member and chair of a wide variety of public and voluntary sector bodies.

John Kingston is the Founder Director of the voluntary sector risk capital fund Venturesome, and is Chair of the Social Investment Market Group. He was Chair of the Institute of Fundraising from 1999 to 2003 and previously chaired two other voluntary sector organizations.

Prue Leith, founder and former Managing Director of Leith's Ltd and a prolific writer and journalist, has been described as "one of the most experienced non-executives in the UK". She currently chairs five organizations including Ashridge Management College, the British Food Trust and 3E's (the first education company to open and run state schools), and is a non-executive director of Omega International plc and Nations Healthcare.

Julie Mellor is a partner at PricewaterhouseCoopers, where her work includes board effectivness reviews in the public sector. Julie was Chair of the Equal Opportunities Commission until 2005. She is on the board of the National Consumer Council and the Employers' Forum on Disability and chairs a young charity called Fathers Direct, a national information centre on fatherhood. She also chairs, for the DfES, a stakeholder group advising on implementation of the 10-year child care strategy.

Gill Noble is a retired senior civil servant. After 25 years working in the Treasury, she keeps herself busy with a number of non-executive posts in the public and voluntary sector, including chairing the St George's Charitable Foundation, an independent charity that holds and manages the charitable funds donated over many years to St George's Hospital in South West London. She has been a trustee of the Meningitis Trust since 1996.

Janet Paraskeva is the Chief Executive of the Law Society, representing and regulating 110,000 solicitors in England and Wales. She is also the First Civil Service Commissioner, Chair of the Olympic Lottery Distributor, non-executive member of the Serious Organised Crime Agency (SOCA) and independent member of the Consumer Council for Water. She has also served as a magistrate and a member of the Youth Justice Board, and has been a non-executive director of a Community Health Trust.

Jane Phillips was, for three years, the Chair of the National Association of School Governors (now part of the National Governors' Association) – an organization that supports, represents and campaigns on behalf of school governors. She has also served on three school governing bodies and twice been chair. Her paid work is in occupational psychology.

Beryl Seaman was Chair of the South Yorkshire Probation Board between 2001 and 2005 and between 2001 and 2004 was the National Chair of the Probation Boards' Association. She is a Commissioner with the Commission for Social Care Inspection and also a Commissioner with the Legal Services Commission. She is Chair of Voluntary Action Sheffield and a trustee of the Camelot Foundation. Beryl has been a magistrate in Sheffield for the past 20 years.

Peter Sherratt is the Chair of Governors of Oaklands Secondary School in London. He is a board member of CAMFED International, Tower Hamlets Education and Business Partnership Ltd and a former board member of Euroclear plc. In his "day job", Peter is the Chief Legal Officer, International for investment bank Lehman Brothers.

Sue Stapely, a solicitor, is an independent communications consultant who works primarily with strategic communications consultancy Quiller Consultants. She specializes in managing the communications of legal matters and on a pro bono basis ran the successful campaign for miscarriage of justice victim, Sally Clark. Sue has served as a board member of the Countryside Agency, Dignity in Dying, the Brighton Dome and Festival, the London Academy of Music and Dramatic Art and the Spare Tyre Theatre Company. Other non-executive board appointments have included the South West Thames Regional Health Authority and the London Ambulance Service. She was the first national Chair of the 300 Group, an all-party campaign to bring more women into political and public life, as well as Chair of the Women for Social Democracy and an elected member of the SDP's National Executive. She is on the Advisory Board of the National Consumer Council.

Geraint Talfan Davies is Chairman of the Institute of Welsh Affairs, a policy research organization, and a former Chairman of the Arts Council of Wales. He has also chaired a housing association and two arts organizations, the Welsh National Opera and the Cardiff Bay Arts Trust. He was Controller of BBC Wales and is now a non-executive director of Welsh Water.

Michael Webber was formerly the Chairman of Pifco Holdings plc, the electrical appliance company. He was also the Chairman of the Industry Trade

Association SEAMA, and Chairman of the Statement of Recommended Practice (SORP) for Charities when he was a Charity Commissioner.

We would also like to thank the following for their participation and support:

Lucy Armstrong is Chief Executive of Alchemists, providing coaching to growing businesses. She is a governor of Northumbria University and a past Chair of the British American Project. She is on the board of an arthouse cinema, the Tyneside, and an active member of Her Majesty's Prison Youth Offender's Institution (HMP/YOI) Castington's Independent Monitoring Board (IMB) alongside her role as a National Tutor for IMB.

Andrew Bridges is currently HM Chief Inspector of Probation at the Home Office. Previously, when he was Chief Probation Officer for Berkshire, he chaired the National Offender Employment Forum.

Lindsay Burley chairs the National Waiting Times Board for Scotland and the Dementia Services Development Trust at Stirling University. She holds a non-executive director appointment with NHS Education for Scotland and is a lay governor of Napier University. Lindsay is a business coach and mediator. Previously she was a doctor, NHS manager and Chief Executive of Borders Health Board in the Scottish NHS.

Robin Burley is the Chair of the Primary & Community Partnerships Committee of NHS Lothian. He is also Chair of the Built Environment Forum Scotland and of the Margaret Blackwood Housing Association. He is a trustee of the Edinburgh World Heritage Trust and was formerly Chair of Elcap, a community care charity. Robin is a business coach, mediator and freelance consultant.

Jonathan Denby is Head of Corporate Affairs for "one" (the train operator for the East of England) and Chair of Arts and Business East. He also chairs the marketing committee of the Norwich Cathedral "Inspiration for the Future" campaign and has previously served on the boards of a number of other organizations.

Paul Edmondson-Jones is Director of Public Health for Portsmouth City Teaching Primary Care Trust and he chairs a number of multi-agency Partnership Boards in the city. He also chairs the National Public Health and

Primary Care Group and the Hampshire and Isle of Wight Public Health Network. In addition, he is a Director of the Portsmouth & South East Hampshire Chamber of Commerce and of Dot to Dot (Arts), which is a Portsmouth-based not-for-profit community arts company.

Joanna Foster is chair of the Crafts Council and the Nuffield Orthopaedic Centre, NHS Trust in Oxford. She is a trustee of the Open University Foundation and recently stepped down from chairing the Lloyds TSB Foundation and the Pennell Initiative for Women's Health in Later Years. She formerly chaired the Equal Opportunities Commission, the BT Forum and the National Work Life Forum and was Deputy Chair of Oxford Brookes University.

Tony Fowles chairs the Lancashire Probation Board. Previously, he has chaired a number of academic and examination boards as well as panels of the Parole Board of England and Wales.

Cedric Fullwood is Chair of the Cheshire Probation Board and a founding member of the Youth Justice Board. He has also been the Chief Probation Officer for Greater Manchester, a member of the government's Task Force on Youth Justice and a Commissioner on Lord Coulsfield's Inquiry into Alternatives to Imprisonment.

Janet Gaymer is the Commissioner for Public Appointments in England and Wales, and a Civil Service Commissioner. She was the senior Partner of Simmons & Simmons until 2006 and the Founding Chairman of both the UK and European Employment Lawyers' Associations. She was an independent member of the steering board of the Employment Tribunals Service and Chair of the Employment Tribunal System Taskforce. She sat on the Council of the Advisory Conciliation and Arbitration Service for six years and is a member of the Council of Justice, having been a member of its Executive Board. She is a member of the Board of the Royal Shakespeare Company and chairs its Nominations Committee.

Arvinda Gohil is the Director of the National Housing Federation, London. In addition, she is a trustee on the Board of Voluntary Service Overseas and Womankind Worldwide, and a Governor of South Bank University.

Maggie Jones is Chair of the West Yorkshire Youth Association. She also chairs a number of regional and national working groups and committees in her role as Chief Executive of the National Council for Voluntary Child Care Organisations. Maggie has over fifteen years' experience of chair and trustee positions in the voluntary sector.

Samantha Mant is Head of Development at Bristol Zoo Gardens. She is also Chair of Governors at Novers Lane Junior School and sits on the Advisory Steering Committee for the Mary Rose Trust.

Theresa McDonagh is the chair of St Anne's Community Services, a housing association and charity based in Leeds providing housing, support and care in Yorkshire and the North East. Theresa is also a trustee and board member of CRASH, the construction industry's charity for homeless people, and of the Wilson and Wilson theatre company. She chairs a number of advisory groups as part of her work for the Joseph Rowntree Foundation.

Bharat Mehta is the Clerk to the Trustees of the City Parochial Foundation. He is a trustee of the Joseph Rowntree Foundation and a non-executive director of North Middlesex University Hospital NHS Trust. Previously, he was the Chief Executive of the National Schizophrenia Fellowship (recently renamed Rethink).

Aaron Ross is the Chief Executive of business consultancy firm Oseko and Operations Director of Health & Absence Ltd. He is the former Chair of the Work Life Balance Trust and previously served on the boards of the Work-Life Balance Advisory Group, Portsmouth Centre for Enterprise and Dreamwall. He has held various executive and non-executive roles in private sector organisations and been involved in enterprise partnerships and secondary school governing bodies.

Albert Tucker is a trustee for a range of charities including Comic Relief and City Parochial. He is a consultant after eight years as the Managing Director of Twin & Twin Trading Ltd, an alternative trade organization. He has, in his career, worked in senior management in the commercial, public and charitable sectors.

Introduction

This is the book that tells you what it's really like to chair: the distilled wisdom of the seriously experienced, the "in their own words" stories of those who combine day jobs with chairing while staying thoughtful, funny, kind, honest, open and above all, despite all, human. Keeping a real focus on the stuff that matters and doing it all without pomposity.

This book is absolutely not the place to find out about the rules. It's not a textbook, but sets out chairs' answers to the questions that are rarely asked: the hard, tough ones, the practical and the fun ones, taking you through the chairing process, right up to knowing when to step down, and the important bits in between, like handling paper-mountains and serious allegations.

Working through the difficult times, admitting mistakes and surviving are all crucial parts of getting chairing right, of leading the kinds of boards that really enable organizations to deliver to the people (or indeed animals or others…) that they serve. Because, when push comes to shove (and it often does), this is all that matters.

1

The big background

What are chairs for?

The chairs' views about this were best summarized by Zenna Atkins: "The chair is there for the people the organization serves, not for the staff or for the board itself or for the chief executive. And as chair, you need to constantly remind everyone on the board that they're there to serve the shareholders or public stakeholders – the tenants, the patients – and not themselves."

Peter Sherratt was equally firm: "The only agenda is the needs of the group of people who benefit from the organization's existence, or suffer if it does a bad job. This is the challenge, and the reason why the board is given its power."

Forgetting that the people served by the organization are all that matters emerged as a big potential trap for chairs, and, as Peter said: "Chairs need friends and mentors to point out when they drift away from this underlying purpose, because it does happen. Chairs have to be aware of that risk not only at the start but throughout their tenure, through arguments or tricky decisions or rivalries."

Chairs also talked about their roles as leaders, both of the board and of the chief executive.

Bill Kilgallon was clear: "Don't duck it, your role is to lead. Lead the board, build the team and lead the organization, focusing on its purpose and priorities." And Deirdre Hutton added: ". . . and lead the chief executive, creating the space for them to achieve their potential."

Peter Sherratt gave some practical tips: "You need to run an effective meeting, inspire people even when it's tough, hire and fire the CEO and articulate a common vision drawn from many different strands." As did Michael Hastings: "The chair needs to set the strategy, the culture and the pace of the organization, monitor all three and make sure the organization delivers to the people it serves."

Chairs talked of times when they lost sight of this bigger picture, forgot their non-negotiable role of keeping the organization focused on what it's there to do and started thinking they were there to defend the chief executive or to keep board members happy. They talked of times when the demands of leadership in their day jobs left them so exhausted that they allowed themselves to take a back seat when their board needed them to be out there leading. And they talked of times when they thought they'd done it all, consulted everyone, decided on the way ahead and handed the "doing" over to the executive, only to find that, months later, they'd not set the pace at which they wanted change to go and very little seemed to be happening. And some admitted to having done this more than once.

Basics of the role

1 Ensure the organization delivers to the people it serves

2 Lead the organization

3 Lead the CEO and create space for him or her to achieve

4 Consult and listen widely, and then take people with you

5 Through consulting and listening, decide the organization's vision, strategy and culture

6 Set the pace required of the organization

7 Set priorities – and non-priorities too

8 Monitor progress, make sure it happens, but don't "do it yourself"

9 Celebrate achievement.

The chair's role – fleshing it out a little

Michael Webber outlined the chair's role in helping to achieve the best results for the organization – there is more detail on the "how" of many of these points throughout this book:

1 Ensure there is an appropriate balance of power between the board and the executive management, with the objective of minimizing the inherent barriers between the executives and the non-executives. The relationship between the CEO and the chair can be the most problematic if each does not understand or is insensitive to the role of the other. Having clear descriptions of the roles of each is important.

2 Ensure there is excellent communication with the board by listening to the non-executives and involving each one of them in all the discussions at the board meetings so that they are signed up to the strategy and the key decisions. This helps make the board into a cohesive team which is a core responsibility of the chair.

3 Keep the board adequately and properly informed at all times on all material issues. There must be a suitable reporting mechanism in place, but one that doesn't involve the board in micro-operational matters. The board's focus should be on the macro and strategic issues, not the day-to-day details.

4 Make sure adequate structures exist so that there is strict adherence to the statutory regulations and governing codes of conduct.

5 Make sure the necessary due diligence and governance procedures are in place so that the accuracy of the monthly and annual accounts can be relied upon.

6 Make sure the board creates a culture of accountability, transparency and operational standards of integrity.

7 Ensure appropriate communication is made to all stakeholders, including staff and the media, in a timely manner.

8 Take responsibility for time and agenda management. These are key parts of the chair's role, alongside concise, even-handed summing up of discussions and the actions that have been decided upon.

What must a chair bring?

Some of these things were clear:

Skills	but not necessarily sector-specific knowledge
Energy	and enthusiasm
Networks	which must be diverse
Distance	to be able to distinguish the important from the trivial
Realism	and insight
Confidence	to be the organization's ambassador

And many of these knit together. For example:

▶ **Skills and distance** – Richard Greenhalgh admitted he knows much less about education than most people on one of his boards, but said his business skills give him a sharper edge. For example: "I know about proper targets, real targets as opposed to government ones. I know about the value of having fewer, outcome based, realistic ones."

▶ **Skills and energy** – Again from Richard, one thing he takes real pride from is: "Being able to move people gently on. I'm not a table thumper or a cage rattler, but I get what we need." Energy will create the momentum needed to move the organization on.

▶ **Networks and realism** – As Prue Leith said: "I have a great address book and my contacts often help us to deliver for the people we serve. But I'm 64 now and I know my networks are ageing so I need to work hard to make sure I keep the boards relatively young and active – we need people who bring diverse skills and we have more and more people who bring much more diverse networks to the organization."

▶ **Skills and realism** – Stephen Falder commented on realism about bringing the right skills: "For example, people want private sector people on their boards, and I hope I do bring business acumen with me. But it's even better when there's a good fit in the scale of the businesses. If you run a business with a turnover of £20 million you may be of less use to a charity for which £500 is a lot of money."

▶ **Distance and realism** – Michael Hastings said: "A big role of the chair is to ensure that the important does not get buried or forgotten in the delivery of the statutory." And Peter Sherratt commented on the importance of keeping a distance from one's own personal agendas, which he described as: "Like ghosts sitting on the shoulders of chairs and board members."

▶ **An ambassador's energy and insight** – Imtiaz Farookhi said: "In the end, one of the important things you bring is your ambassadorial ability. Some think this is about always being the public face of the organization, and in some cases chairs take on this role while others prefer to delegate it to the CEO or another board member. The ambassadorial role goes much deeper and in the end the chair needs to accept that they are the chief ambassador and must deliver on this especially when things get tough."

▶ **And pretty much all of the above** – The chair needs to know the art of the possible, to be able to recognize what can be achieved and what can't and make sure that time isn't wasted on the latter. The need to acknowledge this potential tension was expressed by many chairs of public bodies: while not unambitious, they recommended an element of realism and self-protection.

Prue Leith ended on an exciting, optimistic note: "I try to bring enthusiasm for what's important, while also being firm – polite but bossy."

How should chairs *be*?

You know what you're trying to do, but how should you *be*? What's the "right" way for chairs to behave?

Many talked about "the need to know their place". As Andrew Cubie put it: "The chair has to show leadership, respect for board members and be able to listen to them. You need to have an idea of where you want to get to but not to the point where you can't be influenced around the board table. The chair shouldn't be dogmatic in leadership."

Graham Creelman's story illustrated the value of humility, especially early on: "I was a new chair and had it all worked out, who would do what and so on, even before the first board meeting. So I launched right into it and could see the whole board was scared, as they hadn't really worked out the basics of why they were there. They were truculent, confused, tense and silent. In retrospect, I don't blame them. I got it wrong, pushing for and expecting too much too soon."

John Gardiner's comment illustrated why some executives find it hard to become non-executive chairs, from avoiding stepping on the toes of the CEO to learning the right style for leading board meetings: "You need to be pretty clear just how important and unimportant you are. I call it being the fifth wheel on the wagon. You always need to be on the back, polished and ready to go, but out of the way. When a wheel comes off, you need to be in there, ready, the first one to spot it coming, and able to get in immediately. Then, once in place, you need to be absolutely clear that your main objective is to get out and on the back again. You shouldn't be enjoying being indispensable, you should get out."

Discussions about how chairs should be also touched on levels of independence and perspective, about chairs doing what they believe is right and facing up to difficult issues. Being non-executive made this easier, made them feel more prepared to fall on their swords because being chair wasn't what paid the mortgage. As Zenna Atkins said: "The best chairs are passionate, determined and free." While Stephen Falder added: "You have to give independent credibility to a body, say things others won't, and keep saying them."

And Geraint Talfan Davies reinforced this view: "Executives may be nervous about board reactions, and may be tempted not to bring all the choices to the board, to screen out debate. It's up to you as chair to stop this happening and to tease out contrary views."

Teasing out contrary views

I was recently given the papers for a board meeting and noticed a proposal within them to create a new all-singing, all-dancing customer participation process, but on closer reading it was clear that all customer board members would come off the boards. After general discussion, I pointed out that there might be people who saw this as a retrograde step and asked if anyone had thought about how we might manage the PR. This led to a guns blazing discussion with threats of "over my dead body" and "surely it's the principle" type of discussion. It was good. It encouraged people to look beyond face value.

Zenna Atkins

Chairs also talked about the need to be clear and to be tough. As Prue Leith said: "You must never, ever leave things unresolved. Even if the decision is that X will go away and write a paper for the next meeting, it's far better than bringing back the same problem at the same stage to the next meeting. Never let that happen."

If chairs have to be independent, clear and know their place while being tough, determined and driven, always for the benefit of the people the organization is there to serve, there will be times when they have to follow Simon Fanshawe's advice to: "Lead the organization with vision and enthusiasm but also combine diplomacy with quick wittedness." And they may need to get good at coping with occasional unpopularity and, indeed, frank loneliness.

Here is a pearl of wisdom about how to be from Geraint Talfan Davies, who stressed the importance of chairs looking beyond the board when working this out: "At the Arts Council in Wales, with the CEO's agreement, I sent a note to a wide range of management staff asking for one side of A4 about what they saw as the biggest issues facing the organization. I then went on a regional tour which involved quite a lot of two-hour car journeys with individual managers. You can learn a lot in a two-hour car journey."

And he recalled something that happened when he was running BBC Wales and Sir Christopher Bland was the BBC Chair: "We were all sorted and ready for his visit and the afternoon before, his office phoned up and said he wanted breakfast with 12 staff aged under 35 with no management present. It was such short notice there was no fixing of the guest list and he certainly found out a lot about the organization that way." Geraint approves – he was very clear that chairs finding their way towards how to be must involve talking to people outside the senior management team.

It seems like chairs do need to do a fair bit of hard work, but here are some final words of comfort from Carolyn Berkeley, who said: "Good chairs need a streak of laziness, they are there to make sure others act. On the whole, they need to resist the temptation to sort everything out themselves."

What's in a chair?

Chairs should be:

▶ Open to persuasion

▶ Curious

▶ Modest

▶ Ready

▶ Direct

▶ Brave

Must chairs have first-hand experience of the sector or organization's work?

This question produced interesting answers, with the majority view being that you don't need experience of the sector to be able to chair an organization in it, but that you need a lot else.

Richard Greenhalgh said perhaps, in some circumstances: "You might need a degree of technical know-how to chair a nanotechnology organization." While Geraint Talfan Davies said: "At the Welsh National Opera I wasn't an opera expert, but I knew about the dynamics of creative organizations and the need to balance creative aspirations with financial reality. Without this, I might have taken too long to get a grip on the role." And Bill Kilgallon pointed out: "Be careful about what you consider to be experience. For schools you might think teachers, but surely it should be parents and young people."

Imtiaz Farookhi reckoned that good chairs could cope without first-hand knowledge of the sector: "You don't need it. If you're an experienced operator in any sector you will rapidly be able to see your own strengths and weaknesses and maybe you can cover some of your blind spots with the help of other board members."

Some chairs, however, were positively unkeen on recruiting from within a given sector. As Stephen Falder said: "All first-hand experience is unhelpful because then you come with your own agenda." Zenna Atkins' view was:

"A doctor running a health board may never gain the confidence of other significant staff groups because they're too closely associated with one profession." However, Peter Sherratt's view questioned this: "I guess it's about being seen as fair. People are far too quick to assume that a person who is a doctor represents all doctors. I find this stereotyping offensive."

So, what's the answer?

Richard Ellis focused on the importance of being good at the job: "What you need is the generic skills, leadership, people management and so on. How good you'll be depends less on where you come from and more on how good you are, particularly at thinking outside the box."

And there were words of warning from one experienced chair who says he "blew it". Why? "Because I should have trusted my instincts even when other arguably more 'representative' board members disagreed. I was clear you didn't need experience of the sector to chair a body. Then we came to appoint a CEO and I was swayed by all the board members who did have experience of the sector that the candidate was the right one. So we appointed with me thinking, 'Oh well, leaders must be different in this sector.' I lived to regret my deference and lack of conviction as I spent the following year taking a good person in the wrong job through the performance procedure because of me."

Last words on this to Michael Hastings, who gave perhaps the most pithy advice: "It doesn't matter where you come from, as long as you leave it all behind."

2

Saying yes, saying no

How to decide if you want the chair

First, there is a very practical question. Many chairs admitted that they had made a terrible mistake, for themselves and their organization, because they hadn't thought hard about whether they had time to take it on.

Time

As a rule, add 33 per cent to what the organization tells you will be needed. Then again, be warned that too much is sometimes asked of a chair because whoever's writing the job spec doesn't know the difference between a non-executive role and an executive one and they put things into the chair's spec that are the CEO's responsibility. One of your first tasks as chair may be to sort this out.

Bill Kilgallon was one of several chairs who was clear about making sure you have time for unexpected events: "Do it if you have time not just for when things are going well, but for when things go wrong and the organization needs more from you." While Imtiaz Farookhi added another caveat: "Make sure you've allocated the time for reading the papers, and especially the papers that haven't been written for you and are in a bureaucratic style that is almost designed to confuse you."

And there was an important caution about travel too: make sure you've got time not just for meetings, but to get to offices, across the region or country, to see staff, customers or stakeholders.

Peter Sherratt was clear about not overcommitting: "Don't try to be chair of more than one new thing at a time, give yourself a year to get into it." The other vital questions to ask yourself before agreeing to chair – in no particular order, you have to cover them all – are:

- ▶ Am I or could I get passionate about it?
- ▶ Could I make a difference?
- ▶ To what extent am I doing it because of flattery?
- ▶ How much will I learn?
- ▶ Will I get enough autonomy?
- ▶ Is it do-able?

And the details of these are as follows:

Passion

Only do it if you're sure you can get passionate about the issues addressed, the people delivered to. As one chair said: "Some people can get hugely motivated about setting standards for aubergine cultivation, while others maybe wouldn't. If in doubt, say no."

"You must be doing something you really believe in," said Peter Sherratt, while Bill Kilgallon was crystal clear why he took on chairing the biggest NHS trust in the country and led it through a merger: "I believe the NHS is a vital service. I value it enormously and believe passionately that we can and must go on paying for it up-front as an act of faith. So I'm in it to preserve it and to see it improve and deliver ever better services to people." And he added that it was a tough task that he might not have seen through without the passion, a comment echoed by Zenna Atkins, who says of her NHS chair role: "I'd had little experience of the service, except having two babies and two knee operations. Oh yes, and I think they may have killed my aunt. I didn't want to throw rocks at it but be part of changing it for the better."

Making a difference

Geraint Talfan Davies was very clear on this one: "You must be able to confidently predict that, when you leave, you'll be able to see you made a difference." And he added: "You've got to ask what real value you're bringing, what progress you can bring about, and if you can't see the answers you must say no because there'll always be someone who'll be able to do it better than you."

Richard Ellis agreed: "It's that old cliché, wanting to make a difference. If I see a project has opened, a new partnership has been made, then I know I was right to go for it."

And Prue Leith had encouraging words for those who get stuck questioning their own skills and ability to make a difference, who worry that they need to bring it all, from experience to knowledge: "Knowing you'll be supported by someone good on the board helps enormously. I can look at a menu and it'll jump out at me if there's too much cream or it'll be impossible for the chef because everything has to be in a souffle oven at the same time. On the other hand, I know that nothing ever jumps out at me from a balance sheet, so I'll need a good finance director to help me through that bit, but I might still have a lot I can give in other areas."

Flattery

Prue was also realistic on this one, admitting: "There's an element of flattery. I do ask myself why I'm tempted by a new role, and a bit of the answer is always the glory, feeling flattered to be asked. It's a pretence to say it's nothing to do with oneself."

But susceptibility to this can mean you end up in the wrong place at the wrong time doing the wrong thing, and then messing up, as Geraint Talfan Davies said: "You need to think through what's in it for you, in terms of interest and satisfaction. If you do it for the flattery it won't get you through the long tough and lonely times, when there's not much glory to be had." And Simon Fanshawe was very clear: "Never say yes if you're flattered into it. If someone says they're asking you because you're the only one who could possibly do it, it's always bullshit. Don't succumb!"

Learning

Imtiaz Farookhi said it's all about this: "You need to know you will keep on learning, broadening your knowledge and experience, expanding your networks, taking the learning back into other parts of your life. If you don't think you'll learn much in the role, it will probably begin to bore you and then you'll start boring your colleagues and setting the wrong tone for the organization."

And Michael Hastings warned that you may find obstacles in the way of learning if you've been asked to chair for the wrong reason: "Because the organization is just angling to get your usual expertise, you in our day role, for free. As a result you're not going to learn much." But he also said: "Be clear, chairing is another leadership role. If you don't want another one, don't do it."

Autonomy

This is one you have to look at long and hard and talk to a lot of people about.

Imtiaz Farookhi stressed the need for absolute clarity about autonomy, especially if chairing an organization in the public sector, but also if heavily funded by government in the voluntary sector. As he said: "Before saying yes, be absolutely clear: can you make decisions? Which ones? Your reputation is at risk as a chair, so you need to know what your lines of accountability are."

And one chair, who wished to remain nameless on this one, said: "It's the iron hand of government which makes me run for cover. I won't be a chair where I feel constant bureaucracy on my shoulder, the threat of ill-thought-through budget cuts and the rest." But then again, as Bill Kilgallon said: "Someone's gotta do it!"

The overall message seemed to be dig deep, find out the constraints, and do it if you'll be able to cope with them.

Do-ability

You need to know if it's do-able and then decide. As Bill Kilgallon said: "If you're not sure it's do-able, don't." Geraint Talfan Davies was equally firm: "You'll often see in advance if it's a hopeless task. Some organizations would simply be better off dead."

Listen to the warning voices

I said no to three chair posts. One was a charity that provides advocacy services, and I took one look at the accounts and said no thank you. They were in free fall and going to go bust. I was also asked to chair a local campaign group to improve our local environment for children, but I thought too many people wouldn't want us in their back yard, so I said no, and I was asked to chair the governing body of a local school and said no because there'd be too much bureaucracy and not enough opportunity.

Zenna Atkins

You can never be 100 per cent sure, but you need to be satisfied about three things. Firstly, the organization's money, probity and stability, secondly, with public bodies, you must agree the rules of engagement with government, and thirdly, you go out to dinner with the chief executive. That leaves them with the chance to say they can't work with you.

Richard Greenhalgh

How to spot the poisoned chalice

Some chairs proactively seek them out!

As Richard Ellis said: "One man's poisoned chalice is another man's champagne. Maybe it's actually a huge opportunity you're being offered. Of course you need to ask yourself why they're asking you, but as long as you do the research, and enough research, and are satisfied, then go ahead."

And other gluttons for apparent poison included Bill Kilgallon, who said: "I took the poisoned chalice at the NHS. There was massive opposition to the merging of the two trusts I had to take on, and I knew what I was letting myself in for, but the job needed doing." And Geraint Talfan Davies said: "Everybody told me the Arts Council would be a poisoned chalice. But if you think something is important enough, you should take the risk. I honestly saw it as a challenge to be relished rather than as poison."

But Stephen Falder had a serious health warning: "It's too easy to be arrogant enough to think you can win against all odds. If it's a well crafted poison, you'll drink it and die."

So the crucial thing seems to be knowing how to spot really lethal offerings.

Richard Greenhalgh was confident that: "You'd spot it if you had a good look at the organization." He added: "Poisoned chalices are usually offered amid a certain amount of chaos."

Here are some key ways to spot a poisoned chalice:

- ▶ Look hard at the conditions under which you are offered the role. Is there a sense of calm and clarity, or of undue haste and messiness?
- ▶ Think about how easily you find out what you want to know. As Peter Sherratt said: "Bad is okay, but secret is very worrying."
- ▶ Try to see if there are big conflicts of interest amongst the board members. As Simon Fanshawe said: "Everyone comes with their own agenda and that is the challenge for the chair, but be wary of big conflicts of interest."
- ▶ Assess how ready the crucial players are for change. Inertia can be a strange poisoned chalice, and Geraint Talfan Davies advised: "You can waste time for ages, for years, not getting anywhere, and end up having to go back to square one and rethinking."
- ▶ Find out if anyone's playing media games. As one chair said: "If you have a board member who can, and more importantly decides it's okay to, play out governance wrangles in the media rather than keeping them for the boardroom, it can cause chaos."
- ▶ Finally, is anyone out to get you or confuse you? According to Richard Greenhalgh: "Lawyers and civil servants can be the poisoned chalices. If you come across them, listen with healthy scepticism and always keep your independence of mind."

Can you afford to chair?

This is really three questions:

▶ Can you afford the pay, or lack of it?
▶ Can you afford the time, which is usually underestimated?
▶ Can you afford the exposure, which is seldom anticipated?

Money

You're unlikely to be taking on a chairing role for the money. Many aren't paid, and there's debate about whether public and voluntary sector chairs should be.

Geraint Talfan Davies thought they should: "In the public sector, if you don't pay, how can you expect to meet diversity requirements? How can you expect to provide equal opportunities if you're trying to recruit entirely from people who can afford to do a job for nothing? And anyway, the demands of accountability and compliance mean that chairing is no longer for gents in their spare time. It's different in the voluntary sector."

Imtiaz Farookhi agreed, but for different reasons: "It's right to pay, your performance will and should be appraised, so you should be paid. It establishes clarity about roles and expectations."

Many chairs reflected this view when talking of the difficulties of chairing boards where no one is paid, so they can't be required to turn up. As one said: "When things get tough, you almost have to beg and cajole them to come while they mutter about having to do the things that pay the mortgage first."

But Richard Ellis disagreed: "It's not essential to be paid, you're accountable anyway because you've agreed to do it. There's a real danger in paying everyone for everything. It would be a shame if our society ran only on payment. We all have a responsibility to put back what we can." But he admitted that he wouldn't have taken a chair post were his business not thriving, and Prue Leith echoed Geraint Talfan Davies when she said: "There's always a danger that you'll be just recruiting those who can work for nothing."

The answer? Well, maybe no definitive one, but here are two useful tips:

"Don't be embarrassed to talk about money. You're being asked to do a job, so if you need the money, ask for it."

Simon Fanshawe

"Don't let them pay you and not the rest of the board, as it becomes very divisive."

Jane Phillips

And one chair added: "Don't fall into the trap of making up for the lack of payment with overgenerous expenses. Before you know it, your whole board is travelling around the country first class while the people you serve are queuing for help."

Time

As discussed in the earlier section about how you can know whether or not you want to chair, there are lots of things to consider about how much time it will take. The core ones are:

- ▶ However long they claim it'll take, add a third.
- ▶ Check how much travel is involved.
- ▶ Work out how much extra time you'll need to get up the learning curve, and over what period.

And keep in mind Gill Noble's comment, sentiments reprised by many chairs: "It's no good agreeing to chair because it'll be one day a month and that's it. You need to be confident that you can lead the organization through a crisis too, when you'll suddenly need to take a week to sort something out."

Exposure

You need to look long and hard at the state of the organization and the resources available to you to anticipate and manage any risk to your reputation. Ask to see the risk assessment or risk register, and heed Beryl Seaman: "You need to ask what level of personal responsibility you bear and what the insurance arrangements are on behalf of the chair to cover them if someone sues for negligence. If it's a small organization you might want to take this out on your own behalf. If you're personally negligent, it's just like any other situation – you can be sued." And she added: "This is one reason that I like to keep accurate records of procedures and what's said at meetings. If it all goes belly up, at least you'll be able to show you were acting on good faith." She also suggested that, before taking on a chairing role: "It's worth asking to meet the secretary to the board and figure out how good they are and how well they'll watch out for you."

What do you do if you suspect you're being asked to chair as a token?

From women, black people, middle-class white men who knew they were sometimes appointed because of their religion or because they were gay or because of where they came from in the country, the overwhelming message was "get real".

Imtiaz Farookhi said: "Lots of opportunities in life arise for the wrong reason, if you want to do it, then do it." Prue Leith added: "I'm sure I've been appointed to boards because of being a woman. I don't give a damn as long as they treat me as human once I'm there."

And Geraint Talfan Davies advised: "The people who appointed you might think you're a token, but it's up to you to decide whether you are."

Many chairs were wary of labels. As Stephen Falder said: "I'm a middle-class white man, but not representative of them any more than an Asian leader is of all Asians." And, from Geraint Talfan Davies: "Diversity is more than just skin colour and gender. You need a mixture of people who will see all the angles – what the city will say, what the stakeholders in Scotland will say, what the media will say, and then what all the others will say."

Set against this, many were crystal clear about the need to encourage under-represented groups on to boards and to chair them. As Zenna Atkins said: "With 10 per cent of the population from black and minority ethnic groups, what excuse do we have for totally failing to attract them to our boards?" And Simon Fanshawe said: "It's complex. I don't think I'd want to accept a tokenistic chair as a gay man, but then again I would think about standing aside if a black woman came forward who could do it if I felt that she being black would serve the organization better."

Set against such views, the chairs also cautioned about the dangers of reducing diversity to box-ticking. One gave the example of what happened when the boxes were about race, gender and geography but not religion, and a board serving a totally Catholic community ended up with no Catholic member. Another recalled the board of an Eritrean community centre which was comprised entirely of Eritrean community leaders, despite one of the centre's main objectives being to encourage integration. Both boards could in theory fare fine, but common sense suggested the former might do better with someone from the Catholic faith, while the latter might have found integration easier if it included one or two non-Eritreans.

So, should you chair if it's tokenism? The last word to Bill Kilgallon: "If you feel it's tokenism, you can say you want the job and it's no problem, or you can say no. Don't take the job and then grumble."

Saying yes, saying no – the summing up

The following chapters look at all the questions chairs need to consider about the people with whom they will have to work, the complexities of their relationship with the CEO and the other board members. But before going there, these are key questions a potential chair should ask of others:

1   How much time will it need?

2   What are the financial implications?

3   What state is the organization in?

4   How much independence will I have?

5   How much personal exposure will I have and how am I covered?

6   How ready are the crucial players for change?

And key questions they must ask of themselves are:

1   Am I passionate enough about the organization?

2   How much do I care about the people it serves?

3 Why do they want me?

4 What value can I add?

5 What will I learn by doing it?

6 Do I have enough time to serve the organization in a crisis?

7 Do I have a good enough network?

8 Can I work with these people?

9 Is it do-able?

10 Can I cope with the degree of independence involved?

11 What will I leave behind when I go?

3

You and your CEO

What should the relationship be?

Banish the idea that the chair's task is to "support the CEO". That may be part of it, at times, but the main role of a chair is to performance-manage the CEO.

So, within that, what should the relationship between the chair and CEO be? How did chairs describe this curious, hard-to-pin-down give and take? The most common words and phrases they used were:

▶ **Trust** – All expressed this in different ways and at different lengths, perhaps best captured by Imtiaz Farookhi who said: "No secrets, no surprises, in either direction."

▶ **Edge** – Prue Leith built on the trust idea, saying: "The relationship must be trusting about what's right and wrong, but it must not be cosy, it needs to be challenging and interesting." John Gardiner added: "The relationship has to be 99 per cent supporting, and 1 per cent catching the CEO out." And Imtiaz Farookhi was again very succinct: "The chair and the CEO must not be perceived to be in each other's pockets, even if they are."

▶ **Complementary strengths** – According to Bill Kilgallon: "There shouldn't be rules about who does what, but you should divide up the tasks on the basis of different strengths. You'll waste talent if you have rigid lines between strategic and operational, life's not that tidy. For example, sometimes a chair can be very good with the media while their CEO isn't, or vice versa."

▶ **Shared values** – Bill Kilgallon, again, said: "You must have the same end in mind and common and shared values. If, for example, the CEO is committed to retaining the NHS as a public service while the chair wants to privatize, the relationship just wouldn't work."

▶ **Respect** – Various different kinds of respect were raised as important. Some chairs talked about the need to respect CEOs' space, resisting the temptation to slip into their role, while in exchange CEOs need to respect chairs' autonomy and power. Richard Greenhalgh said he sometimes gets this wrong: "As a chair, I want my CEOs to feel they can come to me, but there is an aspect of this I'm working on. One said to me, 'When I come to you with a problem, it's because I want to discuss, not because I want you just to solve it.'" Another recounted chairing a charity where the CEO was also the founder and couldn't get their head round the fact that the chair could sack them – and they need to respect that!

▶ **Friendship** – Many mentioned it, but they differed on what it meant to them. Simon Fanshawe said: "You need trust and give and take and you have to like each other a lot, and if that stops, one has to go." But John Gardiner viewed it another way: "To be effective, you need mutual confidence and to share some things in common, ethics and a view of the future, but you don't need to love each other. It's possible to hate but still rate each other."

In the end, you have to work together and spend a reasonable amount of time together and rely on each other. So a degree of getting on is helpful.

How is this relationship achieved?

Advice from chairs on how to get the relationship with the CEO, particularly the trust bit, right was:

▶ **Regularity** – While there's no one "right" level of contact, everyone saw regular meetings, formal and informal, as crucial. One chair said he talks to his CEO weekly, is in email contact three times a week, has a formal meeting with them every two weeks and that all this increases in the few weeks immediately before board meetings. Others spoke of regular monthly meetings. Regularity was the word that kept cropping up. As one said: "It's much easier to raise something difficult in a regular meeting that was going to happen anyway, than have to hurriedly fix a meeting because there's a problem."

▶ **Clarity** – This was cited as another key route to the right kind of harmony. Janet Paraskeva set this out with…clarity: "You need to be crystal clear on the different roles of the CEO and the chair. If not, it could be a disaster as you each try to do the other person's role. Make sure you have the two job descriptions and objectives clarified, agreed and written down." Early conversations setting parameters were seen as crucial, and these should be revisited perhaps every six months to redefine the uncrossable lines as the relationship evolves and individuals develop. Janet's idea of a written agreement between the chair and CEO, specifying who does what, was widely echoed: it helps avoid confusion and prevents these two people getting in each other's way.

Here are some other vital bits of chairs' behaviour that were identified:

▶ Send a clear message to the CEO that you are there for them at any time and will drop anything if they need you.

▶ Ensure that the CEO feels happy for you to have access to the other execs, secure in the knowledge that you will never undermine the CEO.

▶ Have lots of robust conversations in and out of meetings, but never any bust-ups unless in private.

What should you offer the CEO?

Zenna Atkins had a very clear starting point on this one: "The CEO needs to know that the chair is prepared to fall on their sword. The chair is dispensable, the CEO much less so."

All agreed that CEOs expect chairs to be honest, available, critical friends, that the rest of the board can and often do provide this input to the CEO too and that the chair/CEO relationship should bring no surprises.

Geraint Talfan Davies commented: "As a chair, it's expected and hoped that you'll bring something additional, something new, not only to the organization, but also to its CEO."

But, CEOs don't want interfering chairs. You know you are one if:

- ▶ you keep snooping around seeking out problems and messes;
- ▶ your CEO tends to walk out of a room when you walk in;
- ▶ staff start bringing decisions to you rather than taking them to the CEO;
- ▶ people seem to be avoiding your calls;
- ▶ your first instinct is to think about how to deliver, not about what needs to be done;
- ▶ you feel you could do a better job than the CEO.

And beware of inadvertent interference. This can emerge in many forms, one of which was described by Simon Fanshawe: "If you're a chair and a volunteer, you need to keep the roles distinct so people don't expect you to be doing one thing when you're doing the other. If, in your capacity as a volunteer, you share an idea with a member of staff without realizing this person would see it as being given an instruction from the chair, before you know it you'll get a big viability paper on your desk when you were only a volunteer bouncing ideas around."

While cautioning against the relationship getting "cosy", Bill Kilgallon said the ideal for the CEO is that the chair "is the person the CEO can talk to off the record, with half-thought-through plans, major problems, for support and advice".

It's all about fine lines, both the nature of the interaction and its purpose. As Imtiaz Farookhi said: "The chair can be useful in conveying board nuances to the CEO and vice versa." Bill Kilgallon added: "The CEO must never expect the chair to toe the party line, and whip the board into doing so, to get things pushed through. This kind of thing can happen if the CEO and chair get too cosy."

Another thing which is vital to CEOs is that their chair is there when the going gets tough. For example, as Andrew Cubie said: "Of course you may delegate dealing with the media to others, but if things become difficult, then it's time for the chair to make him or herself openly available, even to make proactive approaches to the media. If you hunker down, not only do the results tend to be less satisfactory but also you leave others out there in the cold."

The last word on what the CEO wants of their chair must go to Simon Fanshawe: "The CEO secretly hopes that the chair will just go away and shut up. Publicly, they'll say a strong independent chair is essential and that they welcome scrutiny, while late at night with their partner they'll say he's an interfering bastard. Everyone expects the chair to be a champion of the organization, un-blurred by the day-to-day, but all relationships are complex, and this one is no exception."

Chair/CEO cautionary tales

Some chairs' stories of innocence and experience are better unattributed:

"I didn't put in the time at the stage of interviewing CEOs. We appointed the wrong person, and I had to clear up the mess. Next time round I was very clear that all the time spent on the selection process was crucial."

"I was away when the CEO was appointed. When I came back as chair, I found that the CEO was encouraging the board in a view I knew to be mistaken, but his view had become the majority one. I didn't follow my gut instinct, and went with the majority. I just didn't push forward but instead allowed some sort of democracy to overrule. It was a disaster. I picked up the pieces."

"I had performance issues with the CEO, but I let her persuade me that she just needed a deputy. In retrospect, I realize she asked for this to cover all the bits of the job she didn't enjoy. Soon, the CEO was entirely overrating the deputy because she was so grateful at not having to do what she thought were the boring bits, and the deputy gradually became this untouchable person in the organization, not because they were that good but because they covered the tricky bases for the CEO."

"Without even spotting it, the ambitions of the organization were being defined by the talents, or rather, the limits to the talents, of the CEO. He told us what could be delivered and we went with it, rather than thinking through what we should be setting out to do as an organization."

"I inherited a CEO who was appointed by my predecessor, but only for a probationary year. I had read all the books that left me under the impression that my job was to support the CEO through thick and thin. When I realized I was wrong, I sacked him. Then I was told that I had been duplicitous, not just by him but by the rest of the board.

With hindsight, I now know:

- ▶ I should have been managing him from my start.
- ▶ I should have been recording my meetings with him to show that the issues had been on the agenda for some time.
- ▶ I was right not to keep the whole board informed, but I should have discussed it with one or two members, such as the chair of the audit committee.
- ▶ I should have spoken to the stakeholders, not to discuss the issue but to brief them on the decision to get rid of the CEO. In fact, he got to them first."

"When I took over, I found the CEO had lost a lot of confidence as a result of a bruising relationship with the previous chair. I was deeply supportive and generous, and had to then rein in hard later. If you are too sympathetic in the beginning, it may be difficult later when you have to take a harder line."

"I should have followed my gut instincts. Of course I realize that many boards would rather duck decisions if they can, but I knew the deputy CEO was fraudulent, I knew it in my gut, but I allowed other board members to sway me and not investigate. I gave him the benefit of the doubt. In the end it cost us a fortune to get rid of him."

Moving a CEO on

As long as the chair is having regular meetings with the CEO, performance issues will be able to be dealt with over a period of time.

As Zenna Atkins put it: "You should keep your eyes open and forestall problems, never reaching a point where you have to move the CEO on at speed." And Geraint Talfan Davies spoke of the importance of: "Honest appraisal – if it doesn't happen, you're lost. Of course the chair may have to be kind because of the CEO's personal circumstances at a given time, but the interests of the organization come first."

However, sometimes this just doesn't happen, and as Simon Fanshawe said: "The worst thing is not to act quickly enough. It's better to move on a CEO who's ruining an organization and be sued for unfair dismissal than to keep them, slowly taking the organization down with them."

Chairs found themselves in difficult situations over needing to move on the CEO when:

▶ they forget that their loyalty is to the organization not to the individual;

▶ they have inherited a CEO who wasn't managed or questioned by the previous chair;

▶ they haven't had time to find out that things were going wrong;

▶ the targets have been met, but the organization isn't being properly led;

▶ the CEO is doing a good job at hiding the facts.

And they said that things often came to a head less through papers and numbers than through other members of staff expressing concerns.

Richard Greenhalgh spoke of the need, but also the difficulties, of managing CEOs: "If someone is performing poorly, you can first go down the appraisal route and show them they haven't met targets. But if their targets are OK and they're just not building the capacities of the organization, then it's much harder, and becomes very time consuming and expensive to sort out."

And Prue Leith said: "I'm very good with a hatchet, which sometimes means losing chief executives who are simply not right in the job. If you take the trouble, you can often get them to understand this, and help them to go out in a blaze of glory to a new job."

So, here are some practical pointers from chairs who got to this stage of needing to move the CEO on – and decided not to duck it:

▶ Sometimes it helps to give the CEO an executive coach to help them see that all is not well.

▶ Remember, when you are about to share the difficult news with the CEO, they probably know what's coming.

▶ Help the CEO think through how they will brief friends and family.

▶ Share responsibility for the CEO's next step, help them to decide where to go, especially if you appointed them.

▶ Plan the communications, and its timing, to the staff and stakeholders carefully.

▶ Don't become so engulfed by the problem that you delay starting the process of reappointing.

4

You and the board

What should you offer board members?

Peter Sherratt answered this question by describing a response to a difficult situation: "The hardest thing as a chair can be meeting board members' expectations in situations when a decision taken by the board clashes with their view. They need to feel they can have an impact and are being treated fairly. You need to listen, acknowledge their views and articulate the decision in terms of what's best for the organization."

When today's chairs were asked to look back to their days as board members, they described some nightmares – nightmare chairs. And while the list of crimes is pretty long, when chairs recalled these they often said they feared that they might themselves be guilty of the same behaviours. It was a good sign that they felt they were still learning!

Here's their list:

▶ Chairs who did not understand their non-exec role and were constantly interfering with the exec.

▶ Chairs who were also execs and couldn't achieve enough distance.

▶ Chairs who felt they owned the organization and that boards were there to be tolerated.

- ▶ Chairs who never took time to understand the organization or the sensitivities of the other board members, and so were always causing or failing to prevent conflict.
- ▶ Chairs who appointed new board members for personality rather than skills and experience.
- ▶ Chairs who wouldn't make decisions.
- ▶ Chairs who lacked clarity on where the organization was going or what decision had been made.
- ▶ Chairs who were frightened of a weak or even negative board member, and let them set the tone.
- ▶ Chairs who had stopped learning in the role.
- ▶ Chairs who let things stagnate.
- ▶ Chairs who thought that people who think differently from them must be less able.
- ▶ Chairs who thought everything had to be transparent and process-driven.

And suggestions for avoiding some of these? One said: "To be a chair you need to be prepared to be isolated, vulnerable, occasionally disliked and generally thick-skinned." Jane Campbell, though agreeing, added a hopeful, practical note: "The best thing I ever did was to swallow my pride and say I needed a mentor, and she's wonderful!"

Many chairs spoke of the value of pairing up with other chairs and learning from each other, saying this helped to make them more the kind of chairs that board members wanted. Some thought this was particularly useful if they paired up with a chair from another sector because it meant less rivalry and made it easier to concentrate on issues to do with chairing. This approach worked especially well for really experienced chairs who were eager to continue to learn.

So, moving positively on from the nightmare chair list, what did they say the best chairs actually do? They talked about chairs who:

- ▶ get the rules of engagement clear within the board;
- ▶ take time out specifically to build the team;

Rules of engagement for board members

Carolyn Berkeley ran a session for her board which aimed to establish "Rules of Engagement" to which they would all commit. She began by asking:

"You sit down to read your board papers and an item in them causes you concern. Do you:

A   Wait till the board meeting, ask a question which devastates a new executive director and feel you have done your duty?

B   Phone around all your fellow non-execs except the chair and discuss your concerns?

C   Phone the chair and leave it to her/him to sort it out?

D   Discuss it with the CEO?

E   Approach the executive director who wrote the paper?"

The question and suggested answers were phrased in this way to encourage discussion.

A is an unacceptable approach, but encouraged discussion about what *is* appropriate behaviour, and when – what about, for example, an NHS board meeting held in public? It also highlights corporate responsibility and equality of all directors (both exec and non-exec) at the board table.

B allowed discussion about conspiracy/ganging up and when "round robin" approaches are or are not helpful.

C and D reflected the different relationships possible between chairs and CEOs and the extent to which they are hierarchical, trusting or open.

E could arise because you are querying a matter of fact, alerting the author of a paper to questions which may require further information to be available at the board meeting, or warning of strong differences of opinion which could lead to conflict at the board table. In the first two cases, an executive director can handle the questions. In the final example, the chair and CEO need to be alerted and probably need to plan what to do.

▶ seek out the skills, knowledge and diversity needed on the board;

▶ get to know board members well enough to be able to involve them properly and never treat any as token;

- allow people to work in different ways;
- are always crystal clear about who takes on which roles;
- prevent cliques from developing around the topic of finances, by ensuring everyone is up to a shared level of knowledge;
- never pigeon-hole, ridicule or humiliate any board member;
- do all of the above.

Board assessment

The chairs mostly had good experience of formal board assessment procedures and felt they were essential, but not the whole story.

As Prue Leith said: "Assessment needs to be a formal process, 50 per cent interview and 50 per cent group discussion, and sometimes get an outsider to do it."

Stephen Falder warned that formal assessment can be difficult if it's done "to search for weaknesses rather than to identify strengths". He spoke of the value of going beyond the formal, saying: "I was very good at exams without doing any work at school – I know how to beat the system. You need to know how your board members operate for real."

Zenna Atkins couldn't have agreed more, saying: "You can use Belbin or Myers Briggs or any kind of testing, but it's more about talking, listening, getting the feel. You can't just do it through paper, it's the people stuff that counts. See what different people are drawn to, what they say, where they fall short and where they don't. Ask them and other people to describe their strengths, maybe even ask them about their weaknesses."

Bill Kilgallon, who got used to doing annual, formal, individual appraisal of board members, as must happen within the NHS, spoke of the value of meeting one to one: "I have a session with non-execs where I ask for frank appraisal of me, and encourage them to talk about anything that's worrying them. It works. We're honest, raise concerns, and if one has a worry, others usually do too – this process can reveal whether an issue is personal or shared."

Richard Ellis strongly advised assessing the board before deciding whether or not to become their chair: "I wanted to know the board members. I spent one or two hours with each one, and went through structured questions about roles and ambitions which I analyzed on a matrix to pull out views and experience and therefore identified gaps. It meant I had a picture in my mind of the board, their interests and wishes. The CEO did this too and we compared notes."

Finally, given that board assessment is sometimes about the assessment of you, the chair, by them, many chairs now take up Higgs' suggestion (Sir Derek – his 2003 review set out ways corporate boards could and should work better) of appointing a senior director to whom board members can take concerns about the chair. So far, people reported good experiences of this, as Michael Hastings said: "This way, there's a formal questioning procedure in place, which lets it happen without chaos."

Dealing with individual problems

This emerged as being a process within which you may have to work your way through eight main stages, following from the rule that (allowing for subtle variations on how) must never be ignored or avoided. And Zenna Atkins graphically explained why: "If a problem stays hidden, rot will fester and cause septicemia. Get it out on the table and you may be able to grow penicillin on it."

1 Is it you?

Could it be you that's the problem? Ask yourself if you're doing it right. Are you, as chair, failing to motivate people? Talk to people, ask if they're happy and how they could find it more rewarding. Geraint Talfan Davies was very clear that this is the place to start: "Make sure that board members are able to contribute, otherwise you can't tell whether they're choosing not to contribute or are unable to."

2 Is it them?

If it's a problem with a board member, make sure you're not the only person who has difficulties with them, that it's not simply a personal issue between you and them which you need to rise above. But once you know it's not that, then, on the whole, don't ignore it. As Lindsay Burley said: "There can often be a temptation to slide a difficult issue to one side because you don't get on with that board member. But you must take time to see them and deal with it. It's not unique to the chairing role, it's life. That said, it might then be a judgement call; there are some things that, if you leave them, will sort themselves out with time."

And Graham Creelman talked of deliberately letting problems burn themselves out: "I once had people on a board who were meeting as sub-groups outside the board and the CEO wanted to stop them. I let them carry on, and they did, and they worked through their problems."

3 Or everyone?

Make sure it's not a problem with the whole board for which one or two individuals are taking the flack.

As Prue Leith said: "If in fact it's a problem with the whole board, you may need external input, an outsider's view of things. This also tells the board that they have to gee up, and forces them to realize there are real problems." And Imtiaz Farookhi said: "If you find the whole board isn't performing, the board has to take a collective decision about what to do, while you sort out issues of individuals."

One chair added, on a sobering note: "Of course, if you find the whole board is failing and you appointed them and have led them, then you should go."

4 Rogue or spoiler?

So, if you're sure it's not you or the whole board, then you have to deal with a problematic individual or individuals. But first, be sure that he/she/they really aren't useful. John Kingston stressed the need to distinguish rogues from spoilers: "Rogues often bang on and on but sometimes they have a point, and you find yourself coming back to it." Simon Fanshawe agreed: "Even the one who writes daft annoying memos may have their uses, leading you into issues you do need to look at."

But Michael Hastings was tough on spoilers too: "Spoilers really aren't there for the organization to succeed. You mustn't tolerate them as they'll destroy your culture and the team."

5 Air it

Whatever the problem chairs have to tackle, they must keep individual circumstances in mind. As Bill Kilgallon said: "You need to deal with individuals as that. Find out why there's a problem and then see if you can adapt. Do things differently so they stay, or think about them doing something else. Like anyone, non-execs' circumstances can change and you might not know about it."

Richard Ellis added: "If there's a real problem with someone, it may be a case of change their attitude or change them. That said, a trouble shared is a trouble halved, so just bringing a problem into the open can mean you can bring someone successfully back into the fold." And Simon Fanshawe agreed: "Bear in mind that people may perform badly because they're low or in trouble."

6 Clarify the role

Sometimes people simply don't understand their role. As one chair explained: "You may have someone who's been very active at the local level, maybe as a volunteer, and they see their role as ensuring that the organization never loses sight of the local issues. You need to get them to understand about the level at which they are now working, and that their loyalty is to the organization as a whole not to one aspect of it." Another spoke of elected members who remain loyal to another place: "The chair may have to spend time talking through what being on the board means. Say, a board member is also a civil servant and has been elected to the board because their job is linked to one of the programmes being run by the organization. The chair needs to spend time making them understand that they are now responsible for the organization as a whole, not just that one programme. This can be particularly difficult to communicate if the board member is also responsible for one particular funding stream."

Unpicking all this sometimes leads you to discover that your governance arrangements and structure simply don't allow the board to lead the organization. Then you really have to be brave, precise, take a lot of time out to persuade people of the need for change and see it through. David Isaac once had to do this and advised: "You have to know the constitution, what it allows you to do and what it doesn't. You have to talk to everyone, and drive the changes through by using the constitution to support you. Generally people fall into line." In summary, if you're trying to make structural change, you need to know the constitution better than anyone else so that if board members say, "Oh no we can't do that because it violates amendment 7," you can say, "Well actually, it doesn't, for the following reasons." Talk to people, get their thoughts early on, and, as David Isaac said, once you set change in motion, people will generally follow you.

7 Be subtly straightforward

And if Steps 1 to 6 haven't resolved the problem? Then, as Prue Leith said: "Have a quiet word. Usually telling someone you think they're not happy and that you notice they never get their way at meetings and so on is enough to indicate that it might be time for them to go. It'll be the nudge they need."

A nudge they may badly need, according to one chair: "We so often just let people screw up until they hang themselves, it happens a lot."

8 Act

The chairs kept emphasizing that board problems were their problems, that they had a responsibility for seeing and preventing problems, or, if not, for sorting them out. And Carolyn Berkeley illustrated how hard this can be: "Resist your temptation to always make life easier for people. Be blunt. Be meticulous in your approach, appraise, meet regularly, take notes on everything, and slowly get across that there's a problem. But if at any stage they say 'do you want me to resign?' don't instinctively back off. Say yes."

Zenna Atkins was succinct too: "If all the forces are against you, someone is on the verge of an emotional collapse, the CEO or finance director are looking for a new job and someone else's political agenda is surfacing, then get on and deal with it. Don't be an ostrich."

And Richard Greenhalgh said: "GO! Them or you!"

There were also grave warnings from many chairs about the importance of tackling problems – or problematic people – in the ways described above:

"Don't get obsessed with good practice if pragmatic practice is what's called for."

"It may be that they're not underperforming, but they're really out to make the organization fail."

"If you tolerate them on the board, soon you'll find weak members tolerated in the executive team."

"You can skew a whole meeting or decision dealing with one spoiler."

"If you don't deal with one problem person, the rest will resign, slowly but surely."

"One person can bring the whole thing down."

And if you have to get rid of someone, how do you do it?

"Properly," came the resounding reply.

First, every board member should have an individual description of what they're expected to do for the organization beyond attending meetings. Second, every member must be appraised, sometimes by peers as well as by you. And when you discuss the (bad) outcomes with them, ask whether they want to stay and to change. Chairs were clear. As one said: "The secret is formal appraisal, forward, up-front, facing up to people."

While Prue Leith's approach may work (one nudge, and they'll go), getting people back on track or moving people on can take time. And meanwhile? Some chairs spoke of highly effective approaches that they'd seen used to control spoilers in the short term. Not that they could endorse them officially, of course:

▶ Privately acknowledging a disagreement which you couldn't possibly acknowledge publicly.

▶ Setting meetings when certain people can't make them.

▶ Diverting people into time-limited task groups.

▶ Using task groups to divert an issue and the lengthy discussion about it.

▶ Asking someone for a report on a hobby-horse issue to keep them busy.

▶ Meeting with the details person (the person who always reads and cross references everything) before the meeting, and reducing their points from 14 to 2.

▶ Changing a meeting time so that the difficult someone will be too drunk to attend.

▶ Simply, not giving someone much opportunity to speak.

▶ Killing discussion with expressions like, "That's been enormously useful," "We have an awful lot to cover tonight so let's move on," or "Without this kind of passion our board would be nothing, thank you."

▶ Planting a question with a board member to raise an angle or divert discussion.

▶ Deliberately presenting papers with small mistakes in them to divert people from bigger issues.

▶ Scheduling an item that will go on too long just before lunch or just before the end.

▶ Making sure the smell of lunch comes wafting in so that people decide to break.

What to say when . . .

Here are two useful expressions. The first allows you to leave a subject behind without putting it down, the second to create a list for further examination without getting diverted by it on the spot:

▶ "That was very helpful" – will stop someone going on, while not upsetting them or committing yourself to supporting or dismissing their view.

▶ "We must park this one" – will prevent the discussion from going off at a tangent while recognizing that it is a real issue and needs coming back to, but not just now.

Execs and non-execs together

Almost all the chairs said they thought boards worked best when they combined execs and non-execs, and that while their roles differ outside the boardroom, when everyone's around the table, at board meetings, they play the same roles with equal weight. And it takes careful thought and a clever chair to get it working right.

As Stephen Falder said: "The non-execs mustn't get into business detail and micro-management." Reflecting further on the distinction, Simon Fanshawe reprised Stephen's comment when he said: "Building the framework is the board's job, exec and non-exec, while actioning it is for the execs."

So, given the role of execs outside the board, to implement the board's decisions, problems arise when execs at meetings don't behave as board members, but behave and respond to issues as execs. This can lead them to get into delivery issues at meetings, leading the non-execs down this path too. As Zenna Atkins put it: "Execs shouldn't be talking about the intricacies of sorting out the waiting lists at the board meetings, they should be operating alongside the non-execs and looking at the bigger issues, being the conscience of the place."

And it can become a really circular problem if there are non-execs on the board who are itching to get into the detail and, because the execs are there, they have all the information to be able to. Again from Zenna Atkins:

"Before you know it, the non-execs and then the whole board are into the 'how'. It's often very difficult for people from business, with their strong desire to meddle in business planning, to resist meddling. If you're confident that the 'how' will work, that the executive has produced a good business plan and are getting things done, shut up and get your board out of the details."

Getting execs and non-execs working well together on the board, and not concentrating on building or supporting one group at the expense of the other, is certainly a tough call for the chair. Indeed, as Imtiaz Farookhi pointed out, you may need some help: "All this is not intuitive and if you have inexperienced board members you may need to put some time and money into training the execs and non-execs to work together."

Finally, a word of caution about the make-up of your board and the importance of thinking about who's really needed on it. As Zenna Atkins said: "There are lots of different board structures, and you need to have clarity about what structure is best for you. Will you have all the directors, or just the CEO and finance director? Ask yourself what the difference is between your board and the senior management team. It can be a real muddle and waste of time and money moving everyone round to meetings all the time. If all your directors are regularly flying from Edinburgh to Bristol for board meetings, you have to ask yourself whether maybe they don't all need to be board members, but could just attend when needed."

What is a diverse board, and how can you get one?

There was a big plea here for abandoning formulae – which were seen as all too often shallow and failing to produce either real diversity or a successful board – and replacing them with strong commitment from chairs to actively widen the pool.

Deirdre Hutton explained well why formulae may not work: "If you recruit people so you can tick traditional diversity boxes and not because they're great and bring new skills and perspectives to the board, they sometimes think they've been appointed as representatives. This produces difficulties because boards are about strategy, accountability and monitoring, and seldom work if they are about representation. A member in a representative role is often caught between representing a group and making the best decision as a board member for the organization."

Michael Hastings was very clear that: "Diversity is about the board that can understand all the issues and angles." He added: "You need to keep to the competencies, including HR, marketing, legal, financial, commercial and so on. Then you need to make sure you've got the competencies about seeing the issues through the eyes of different stakeholders, whether that is the private sector or disabled people or religious groups or government."

Prue Leith picked up on this idea of not thinking diversely enough about diversity. As she said: "So many boards don't include an HR director, yet the organization goes on about how people are their most important asset. And what about headteachers? A head or college principal will have run organizations with 1,500 children, 300 teachers and huge budgets, while taking and evaluating risks. They do all this for their living, yet most boards ignore their skills." And Richard Greenhalgh said: "Diversity is the big issue, isn't it? But it's about richness of ideas, experience, skills, background, ability, while its outward manifestations are gender, race, disability, age and so on."

Imtiaz Farookhi's comments echoed this, when he said: "Diversity is contextual. If you're providing certain services in an inner city context and the whole board is white guys in suits, then the nominations committee isn't doing a good job. But if you're some committee designed to debate atomic structure, then you need to have the people who know about that."

Bill Kilgallon took the challenge of ensuring diversity further, pointing out that: "Your criteria may be excluding people. The NHS board that looks for people with experience, who hold senior positions, perhaps have been carers, by default excludes a man of 28 who's never been in a senior position and hasn't yet been a carer but who may have a valuable perspective and a vision which is vital for the organization's future. It's not conscious, but it's exclusion by default. You need to keep thinking it through; young people are needed, they bring a questioning eye."

So, what should chairs be doing to widen the pool?

Prue Leith was clear: "You need a formal process for discussion within the board to check out gaps, chart these, work out what the organization needs, recruit to fill the gaps and accept no excuses that people are too hard to find."

Many chairs also spoke of the value of networking, as one said: "Doing some active work yourself, meeting people, remembering them and encouraging them." But Prue cautioned: "Of course, there's the danger that an old chair like me will recruit an old board because those are the people I know." But she added, reflecting her previous comments about formal processes: "Then again, you're not the only one doing it and you are consciously going out to make sure you don't recruit in your own image."

Echoing Prue, Richard Ellis said that ensuring diversity is a big undertaking: "In the government-led organization that I chair, I have to have a wide range of board members. Diversity is expected across race, gender, age as well as regions, and the organization encompasses six counties. It's an incredible matrix and you never get it right. You have to work hard to get the right people to apply, advertise, formal search, but also keep your eyes and ears open for new people. I keep lots of business cards for the future."

Deirdre Hutton was very clear about the need to branch out: "There's a real danger of appointing boards where people are too much the same, they think the same. You need people who'll think differently, produce trouble, rock the boat, and you must allow them to do so." Andrew Cubie agreed: "People around corporate board tables are often of the same mould. Public and voluntary sector boards often have far greater diversity of backgrounds and experience and if they work well they produce much richer outcomes." But he also struck a note of caution in relation to ensuring you get the best out of them: "What you can't do if you chair a diverse board is conduct the meeting as you would a corporate one." And Richard Ellis agreed: "You have to keep the jargon and acronyms and other incomprehensible language out, otherwise, having recruited this fantastically diverse board, they'll decide it's not for them and leave."

Peter Sherratt picked up on this too, saying: "You have to take real time out to understand the new perspectives yourself and learn new languages and approaches, or you'll appear unwelcoming to new members. It's key for chairs to elicit views and not just wait for people to shout out, to be aware that different cultures produce different levels of extroverts."

And, as Carolyn Berkeley said: "Seek out diversity as a strength, and then enjoy it!"

5

The practical stuff

Running meetings

Four things are crucial to good meetings: preparation, timing, tone and momentum. So, here's a closer look at each of these and at how to handle them.

Preparation

Deirdre Hutton made a strong point about how most of the chair's work is done outside meetings: "You need to be very clear about this, but don't fool yourself. Meetings are crucial and if they go wrong you'll have to put a lot of time and effort getting back on track." And she elaborated: "As you leave the meeting, don't think 'great, nothing to do till next month' because much usually needs to be seen through between meetings. This is the time when the chair needs to talk to people, take soundings, do the groundwork on issues due to come up, understand individual board members' positions. This isn't about stitching up people and issues, but about getting yourself best placed to lead the discussions ahead."

Under the preparation topic, chairs also talked about papers, room layout and all the little but crucial things, detailed under "tips", next.

Tips on preparation

- ▶ Make sure the food is good, although this doesn't necessarily mean expensive.
- ▶ Vary the venue.
- ▶ Be ready when others arrive.
- ▶ Make sure the room and chairs are comfortable.
- ▶ Change the table if it's the wrong one, too big, too formal, and in particular avoid long thin ones where you can't see everyone.
- ▶ Make sure you reserve a seat for yourself in the centre.
- ▶ Prepare crib-sheets to remind you who everyone is and what their interests are.

Timing

Getting the board to stick to time can be really tough.

Peter Sherratt said: "Start the meeting by setting the pace. Try something like, 'We have a lot to get through this evening,' and never hand over to a speaker without putting the word 'brief' into his or her introduction."

Reflecting on the chair's responsibility for getting the timing right, Stephen Falder said: "I can be rude in that respect," adding that "indeed, before you know it you'll have allowed Ms X to tell the story about the time the mouse got trapped in the video recorder when you're in the middle of sorting out agenda item 7. This is not to say you shouldn't encourage anecdotes when not keeping strictly to time, but be careful when you should be."

And if it all goes wrong and you're left needing to be fleet of foot because something you hadn't anticipated needs more time, stop the meeting and get agreement on what items will be dropped, while being aware of people who may be waiting outside to present their piece.

Tips on timing

- ▶ Make sure board members can meet the CEO informally outside the meeting on issues of detail or clarification.

▶ Allow time for people to test out ideas informally or during the meeting so that they don't all appear under "any other business".

▶ Know the agenda, know what has to be decided, what can be deferred and where the discussion and debate are likely to happen.

▶ Put timings against agenda items if this helps.

▶ Give presenters clear briefs on timing and on what you want covered, especially how much background you want them to spell out.

▶ Arrive early so that people can talk to you.

Tone

Simon Fanshawe said you must deliberately make it enjoyable: "Make sure people laugh at some points in the meeting, get through the business, don't ever be afraid to get interesting discussions going and give them time. Let things happen." Richard Ellis added: "Get things going, don't let it get turgid, or let people get stroppy, use humour, but make sure it's not just you making the jokes."

Simon Fanshawe was very passionate about this issue because he says otherwise people start not turning up to meetings at the end of long days: "Have tea and cakes before the meeting, dinner afterwards, set board members interesting targets and above all don't take yourself or anything else too seriously."

One way of making sure things stay sensible, that the tone doesn't get pompous? Nice advice from Geraint Talfan Davies, who said: "I always admired Richard Hooper, the deputy chair of OFCOM, who used to fine board members every time they used a word that was unnecessarily long. It always broke the ice and there was a saucer of coins by the end of the meeting." And Bill Kilgallon added, in a similar vein: "I insist on no jargon or acronyms. I refuse to learn them and stop the board from using them. NHS is the only one I'll allow, and even that only just!"

Finally, an important aspect of tone was about getting to understand your board members and ensuring they all have a sense that they can be heard and make the points they want. More tips on this follow and, as Michael

Hastings said: "Be careful of developing 'ways of doing things' which can feel very excluding, especially to new people."

Tips on tone

▶ Hold meetings in a cheerful room with natural light.

▶ Smile: the chair mustn't look grim.

▶ Celebrate from time to time, have some lighter items on the agenda.

▶ Make sure all the board members have targets and tasks.

▶ Thank people, congratulate them, enjoy and share each other's successes.

▶ Identify the people you can tease and do so if the meeting becomes too serious.

▶ Cope with moments of silence at meetings, don't feel you always need to fill them.

▶ Show you're enjoying the meeting yourself and have been looking forward to it (whether you have or not).

▶ Don't hog the platform, usually express your views after others, unless a minority view needs to be allowed to be aired and expressing your interest may facilitate this.

▶ Don't be too provocative as this may silence others.

▶ Make sure everyone feels comfortable about getting up at the meetings to stretch their legs, get a drink, go to the loo.

▶ Watch people's body language. For example, someone who sits up, builds up and then settles back may have wanted to say something useful. Maybe you need to give them the space to talk.

▶ Use first names, but make sure you know them.

▶ At the end, thank everyone for the time they've spent at the meeting.

▶ Keep a close eye on who contributes and on what issues, so you can talk to board members who might be becoming single issue contributors. But, set against this, recognize areas of special interest and value.

Momentum

This was a tricky one because sometimes you need to slow it down, while at other times you need to do the opposite.

As Richard Ellis said: "You may need to keep your own momentum in check." Similarly, Prue Leith said: "I'll make the wrong decision because I want to make one rather than lose momentum. I'm impatient, I like action. I've got a cabal of execs and non-execs who I can really trust to tell me to slow down."

Stephen Falder said of momentum: "How to stop momentum is hard, stopping people doing what they've always done, and resisting constant blind pressure to move on." Overall, there was a strong feeling that ill-thought-out momentum was an easy trap and one which led to important things being missed: too much remains at a superficial level, opportunities aren't spotted and it's hard to create the desired culture within which anyone can say anything.

But then again, some chairs longed for momentum, recalling times when things stagnated: "During big change programmes, you need to keep the pressure at a reasonable pace in order to gather the momentum to get through them," said Bill Kilgallon. And one chair talked about: "Creating burning platforms to generate a sense of urgency and pace." One useful technique for this was suggested: "Invite in outsiders. They can be heard when an insider can't be or won't be understood, and can keep things moving."

Geraint Talfan Davies said of momentum: "It needs real thought. It's about being precise about where you're going and what the milestones are. You need to build in room and time for self-criticism and keep in mind that small incremental steps may be right sometimes, while at other times you need to lob a pebble in the pool and produce some uncomfortable ripples."

So, while momentum needs to be on your agenda as chair, the direction in which you're pushing it is a judgement call. When you think you've got it right, as Simon Fanshawe said: ". . . then change it". There were also wise words from Richard Greenhalgh: "Momentum? It's the biggest challenge isn't it, especially when you're spinning lots of plates at the same time.

There's no secret, just don't try to be the only source of momentum, don't feel that you've got to do it all yourself."

Tips on momentum

▶ Sort the order of the agenda to provide interesting mixtures of issues and pace, and change the order during the meeting if needed.

▶ Don't take anything to the board you don't want them to decide on.

▶ Don't leave essential decisions unmade.

▶ If a decision has to be deferred, think about whether the question can be advanced in some way before the next meeting so it doesn't come back on the agenda at the same stage next time.

▶ Spend time summarizing and clarifying, but also give people a sense of making progress and producing outcomes.

Things I wish I found easier

Making that judgement of whether to go with the flow or take a stand and provide leadership.

Julie Mellor

Getting the timing right for the summary, so that when you've completed it someone doesn't make another point.

Deirdre Hutton

Keeping focus and discipline. Sometimes there are lots of opinions and I know we don't have to make a decision now and so I allow things to get muddy – and then someone says, "Can I be clear what we have just decided," and I know I've lost it.

Prue Leith

I find it difficult to tolerate discussing things if it adds nothing to the decision – if we've already effectively concluded on an item and people want to keep talking. But I've come to realize that sometimes I have to let discussion carry on because people need to feel they've had their say.

Zenna Atkins

Paperwork

"People write at such length about so little. There's loads of stuff I don't read," said Simon Fanshawe, while Imtiaz Farookhi was firm about who must control this: "It's the chair's task. You have to be ruthless about what you want, your job is to sift out the relevant 1 per cent of paperwork amongst the humungous amount received."

He singled out civil servants producing papers for public sector boards as special villains: "They don't treat the board who will receive the papers as customers, and they should." And Richard Ellis agreed: "If I say one page of A4, then the bureaucrats say 'okay' and change the font size!"

Pam Chesters gave clear advice: "Agree a standard format that makes it clear what the board is being asked to do with the report, keep the expectation that it will be concise and stand on its own without further detailed explanation, which will be confined to appendices for those who wish to see them. List a named executive member to whom detailed or non-strategic questions can be addressed prior to the meeting."

Richard Greenhalgh suggested trying hard to get: "Someone who can read and summarize for you. Not a PA, but someone who doesn't ask what it is you need to know, but who knows, and is very good on the internet."

Deirdre Hutton said: "The paperwork provides a real health check of the board. The shorter the paper, the better the discussion." She added: "Good boards have great papers to read. If you get a bombardment of papers with no big picture, assume the execs are lazy, unfocused or, worse, trying to mislead you."

Prue Leith said: "I really resent the 10 kilos of paper in my backpack that I don't need to carry to the meeting." And because this was a sentiment that was widely shared, here's a recipe:

The Prue Leith and Friends Recipe for Perfect Paperwork

▶ Keep it succinct, set out as narrative, analysis, options. Decisions can be based on these.

▶ Avoid tabloid-speak as well as acronyms, medical, technical and financial jargon.

▶ Send back any paperwork that contains acronyms or jargon and ask board members to do the same.

▶ Keep paperwork down. In the meeting, you can discuss a one-side paper and tell the board: "There's a huge file behind all this, if you'd like to know more".

▶ Too long may be a lazy executive – be strict about saying shorten it.

▶ Ensure that any risks are clearly highlighted.

▶ Two pages of A4 per paper, max. Any more, put in appendices.

▶ Sending print-outs of slides to be shown at a meeting can unnecessarily increase the paper load, especially if there are only a few words on each slide.

▶ Ask the board annually if the paperwork style is okay.

▶ Don't land the board with two inches of paper on Saturday for a Monday morning meeting. They may not want to lose their weekend to it.

▶ Papers should always go out a week or more before the meeting, unless there's a merger or serious ongoing issue. Only small financial updates may need to be sent on at the last minute.

▶ Email is useful, but don't email board papers – it'll clog up home computers when what people really want is emails from grandchildren in Canada.

▶ Before a meeting, go through the papers and colour-code key points that reflect different lines of action. This means you'll be able to steer people neatly through the arguments and stop them getting on a uni-directional roll.

And after the meeting? On minutes, there were many warnings. As Richard Greenhalgh said: "Make sure your minutes are action reports, not verbatim accounts. The test is when you say 'any comments?'. In truth, if the board has received action points, they'll have looked at them hard. If they're minutes, no one's read them."

Imtiaz Farookhi agreed: "Minutes must be an *aide-mémoire*, a record of decisions, not a great long archive of arguments and points made." And as one chair pointed out: "If you allow verbatim minutes to be produced, you give free rein to the bores – either those who are on the board or who are speaking to it – who'll go on and on at the meeting so that they get their points into the minutes."

But not into Stephen Falder's minutes, as he said: "I've managed to get minutes decreased from 13 pages to an executive summary, or to action points where it's clear who's going to be doing what, names dates and benchmarks."

Finally, another Prue Leith tip for coping with what can sometimes be a truly insurmountable paper mountain: "If you're a school governor, there's no way you could read all that the DfES sends you, but you may find you can get all the information you need from the relevant trade or sector publication that tells you what's going on in it."

Things you can't put off

▶ Checking the minutes, said Beryl Seaman: "Otherwise some action point may get through that someone will quote back to you later on. This is an important part of reducing the risks of chairing, especially in the public sector."

▶ Understanding the finances, said Prue Leith: "Some chairs think they can delegate the finances to the treasurer but actually they need to take the time to understand them thoroughly themselves. Especially if, like me, finance is not their skill."

▶ Bringing the board together, because it may be comprised of people from individual organizations brought together for historical, geographical, scale or whimsical reasons that no one can remember and may not make pure strategic sense. On the whole, the temptation is to leave things as they are and muddle on, but chairs do need to take time to build links, clarify agreements and, most importantly, decide the values that all board members will sign up to. This is even more relevant for group boards with members who are subsidiary boards, where perhaps the subsidiaries have different understandings about the role of the group.

▶ Doing the spec for the sub-committees. One chair admitted delight at creating a sub-committee so they didn't have to go into the detail of the stuff they found tedious. While not a disaster in itself, they also admitted not taking the time to get the brief for this sub-committee right, and that mattered. Another chair admitted to realizing that, having created an HR Policies Subcommittee, she failed to notice the word "and" had been slipped in between the words "HR" and "Policies". An innocuous sub-committee had become an HR and Policies Committee and saw its brief as being just about everything to do with the organization.

▶ Keeping an eye on sub-committees. If they exist, chairs mustn't discover too late that they've extended their brief or changed how they've decided to operate.

▶ Asking the difficult question. "It's easy to defer the unpopular or the boring. Don't," said Michael Hastings.

▶ The small, but important, things. As Geraint Talfan Davies said: "If it matters and you put it off, you'll soon know it. What I really regret putting off is the small, human things. That note I didn't write to someone, the pat on the back I didn't give. It's those things I kick myself about if I leave it too late to do them."

But finally, Zenna Atkins did say that chairs need to get real, and to recognize that some things have to be put off because they just can't be done. As she said: "Put off the unwinnable battles. If there's a problem, there's a solution. If there's no solution, then it's a fact, so live with it."

Golden rules on sub-committees

✓ Appoint the chair

✓ Produce a clear term of reference

✓ Keep a close eye on them, but . . .

✓ Don't meddle

✓ Have as few as you can

✓ Make them time-restricted

✓ If you have to have standing sub-committees, do an annual review to ensure they serve their purpose, but . . .

✓ Close them down when the job is done

✓ Remember that you can re-call one

✓ Set deadlines for all sub-committee projects

✓ Remember their importance in risk management

✓ Watch out for overlapping agendas on sub-committees – make it clear which one is doing what.

Facing up to the media

When the media are breathing down your neck, you have no choice but to deal with them. Sue Stapely shared some wisdom about the best techniques:

1 Get the bad news over with – admit it, and quickly. This limits the damage.

2 Don't delay – you won't be in charge of the timetable, but . . .

3 . . . Take charge where you can – establish a clear and simple decision-taking process – don't let the media catch you out.

4 Know your facts – and get the case straight.

5 Check the law, but . . .

6 . . . Don't forget common sense – the human touch.

7 Cover your back. Don't cover up – you must be seen to have done the right thing.

8 Remember: Reputation, Reputation, Reputation.

9 Remember **all** your audiences – a balancing act.

How do you know what you don't know?

This one's easy, said Prue Leith: "You don't really understand what you're hearing or what you're talking about."

Knowing what you don't know was seen as being about taking the time to stop and think and listen and hear what others are saying to you, or even things you may be saying to yourself but not listening to. Most chairs said that nine times out of ten when they felt they'd been hit by something totally unexpected, it was because they'd been distracted elsewhere and weren't putting in enough time. Or indeed, they had *felt* it coming but failed to *see* it clearly enough until the last moment.

Geraint Talfan Davies said: "Read, listen, visit – keep your eyes open." Richard Ellis elaborated: "Take time to reflect. The strap-line for the region where I chair the development agency is 'space for ideas', and certainly, quiet reflection, closing my eyes and mulling things over, creates the time when I realize what I don't know."

Not feeling a fool for not knowing was seen as really important too. As Peter Sherratt said: "There's a very direct American phrase for this, 'Be smart, be dumb.' Have the bravery to ask very simple questions without fear, without worrying about losing face. Even sometimes ask questions you know the answer to on behalf of the rest of the board." Stephen Falder agreed: "When I do ask the stupid question, I know I'll be doing so on behalf of 90 per cent of people who didn't understand what it meant either but were afraid to say so."

And one blind spot that Pam Chesters said was all too common is financial: "Never assume that all the board members understand even the basics of the organization's finances. They don't, and often they don't ask enough when they are new because they are working their way in, and then they feel they've been around too long to ask without feeling stupid. Plug the knowledge gap with a targeted teach-in. This breaks down the feeling that financially literate people are part of some inner sanctum on the board, and you'll then get much more effective contributions from those members who previously took a back seat when things with serious financial implications were being discussed."

One important caveat to all this was pointed out by Bill Kilgallon, who stressed that you don't need to know it all: "If you're chairing an NHS trust but don't have a medical background, there's masses you won't know about medical life and strife. Indeed, maybe that's why you were appointed, for your distance, for the other things you bring to the board and the organization." Imtiaz Farookhi agreed: "It's the Donald Rumsfeld thing about known knowns, known unknowns and unknown unknowns. You have to work on your blind spots as well as understanding there are things you don't need to know."

What can you expect to achieve?

Simon Fanshawe made a nice point about this: "There are no limits, but you have to make ongoing realistic assessments. When I was a comic, if I had a joke which I knew was laughter size 6 and I gave it laughter size 10 delivery, it would get laughter size 3. Don't limit your ambitions, but assess, and make change gradual, even if you're impatient."

The chairs saw huge potential for their organizations and had huge ambitions for them, and for most, a key challenge was that of setting the right pace. "Pace" was a word many used, and many spoke of boards that set objectives and strategies and then handed over the task of delivery without thinking long and hard about pace. And this then limits achievement. As Richard Ellis said: "You know things aren't going well when the balls are always in the same place."

And if things begin to stagnate, if you really feel you're not achieving. What then? What's the most likely cause?

▶ **Overestimating** – As Stephen Falder said: "You have to know your scale and do something that fits within it. You can be successful without becoming world-famous or causing massive disruption. Know your place in the market place and influence it appropriately." And, from, Zenna Atkins: "I had to ground a very welfar-ish board to accepting that they were not the change agents of the universe but a small local support agency which could do great things but not everything."

▶ **Underestimating the timeframe** – Chairs talked about realistic evolution rather than revolution, and giving it long enough. As Michael

Hastings said: "Time is needed for change, especially in big organizations, and the better you do the change the more effective it will be." Having said that, he cautioned: "But don't use needing time just as an excuse to delay. Aim high."

▶ **Fighting on too many fronts** – As Richard Ellis said: "There are only so many fronts you can fight at one time. Not getting too limited by this means having enough good people around who can pick up the balls and run with them."

▶ **Failing to spot what can't be changed** – "There will always be limits to the board's power. Make it clear to members what these are, and don't waste time on issues it can't affect," said Zenna Atkins.

▶ **The executive** – The chairs were clear that you may need to look hard at the executive. If there's a logjam, it might be here, a member of the top team or the CEO. They agreed that the big limiting factor is usually the quality of the executive, and it's the chair's job to face up to this one. As Bill Kilgallon said: "On one occasion I didn't spot weak second-tier staff, those reporting to the directors, and allowed the development of a programme that the next level couldn't deliver. It's the CEO's role to assess the capacity below the board, but the chair is involved too."

▶ **Money** – On a sobering note, Geraint Talfan Davies said: "It's often lack of money from government which curbs public sector bodies, but it pushes you to prioritize."

6

The difficult stuff

Changing things

Chairs were asked about breaking the mould – how they do it, when and why. Some spoke of setting to with pneumatic drill and industrial blow-torch, others about chipping away with varying degrees of tenderness, while some favoured keeping radical change for really extreme situations and trying instead to promote or rebuild a status quo. And, as several pointed out, what you do and when is mainly about where the organization is and what's needed. One described this as: "The seasons of the organization. What it needs now may be very different from last year or the next quarter."

Richard Ellis reckoned chairs don't on the whole break moulds but instead create the circumstances where others can: "You need to be convinced and convincing about your beliefs, helping others to go over, around, under hurdles. Get out there, convey the need for things to change, for moulds to break, give people permission, and support them through it."

So, how can you send a message that conveys the need and permission for change?

Michael Hastings said: "There are moments, very rare moments, when you break the rules. You allow or even encourage the rows, you bend the procedures, you do what you shouldn't do, like springing things on the board, and you do it because there's a compelling reason why sticking to the rules would mean never getting the organization to deliver what it should to the people who matter. But you only do this very rarely, as an exception; do it too often and you'll produce a culture of mistrust. You have to maintain the values of the board and if you're regularly producing exceptional circumstances in which you need to break the rules, those values and the trust will begin to seep away."

Richard Greenhalgh added: "People don't believe you anyway if it's always happening. If for example I let fly at a meeting, it's so rare it's incredibly effective."

And change does indeed sometimes need to be really radical. Zenna Atkins talked about when she became Chair of the NHS Primary Care Trust in Portsmouth: "I ignored the current trend in the NHS and dismantled all the committees that weren't statutory, the ones we didn't have to have by law."

She went on to explain why: "It's easy to fall into having committees because it's what's always been done or seems like a good idea. But people not committees make things happen, and by backing people not structures you get real accountability, speed of decision-making and a fluid and successful organization. By backing committees you often get no decisions, fudged accountability and a moribund organization. Getting glued down with bureaucracy kills a board and can take down an organization, and it's up to the chair to get the right balance. Boards die a slow miserable death if they become obsessed with evidence, reports, process and recording. You're in the business of delivering something, never lose sight of that, and if people want to keep doing things just as before, stand firm and shake them up."

Standing firm and shaking up sometimes needs a bit of passion from the chair to unite the board. As Simon Fanshawe said: "You need to make a critical mass of diverse forces work together. Think of the great roaring social movements. They had pride in what they believed in, a point to make, and just got on with it."

Geraint Talfan Davies told a stirring story about how he spread a vision to create the necessary passion when he became Chair of the Welsh National Opera: "The company needed to get all four parties in the new Welsh assembly on side. We knew that not every member liked opera. Some came to performances. Some didn't. But we also took everyone through the scenery workshops, where painters, carpenters, ethnic trainees, scores of people were building sets, some destined for Covent Garden, some for Chicago. They saw jobs, skills, exports, saw how important it all was, and there wasn't a single vote against what we were doing."

Peter Sherratt expressed concern about chairs who try to shake things up too much. Focusing on the phrase, "You can't make an omelette without breaking eggs," he said: "I hate the phrase. Change can be easy and fun. Wind up the clock. You can't see the hands move. Look back five minutes later and you've moved on. The best way to wind up the clock is to articulate a vision people buy into and let change tick along to that agenda."

But Geraint Talfan Davies reckons it can be tougher and said: "It's not always easy, you have to excite people with the process of change and the prospects it holds. Some just don't want it." And indeed, most chairs had dealt with board members who didn't see change as necessary, which was difficult: while they had different approaches to achieving it, the chairs saw change as being what the role is all about. As one put it: "If things aren't changing then you're not doing your job."

So does that in fact mean breaking eggs? It certainly may mean persuading the forces behind stagnation to move on or out, and Geraint nicely summarized by saying: "Careful co-operative change does not have to be mutually exclusive with breaking eggs. It's not 'either we work by consensus or we break eggs'. It's possible to do first one then the other, or to alternate."

One of the biggest problems surrounding change seemed to be what to do when the organization appears to be doing okay, but is failing to look to the future. According to most of the chairs, most organizations benchmark their success by what has come before, rather than where they could go. To make change happen, the chair needs to be brave, which can be really hard if the other board members are complacent and not up for taking risks. As

Michael Hastings said: "An organization might have a fantastic reputation but its figures are on the way down and the finances long-term don't look good. To rescue it, you may have to do things others consider overreacting. You as chair have to bring the energy to make the changes."

The last word on change goes to Prue Leith, who said: "It's about cutting through the crap and being seen to do so, cutting through the waffle to get to the meat." She added: "It's especially true in the public sector and the charity worlds and in education. It's as if they're afraid to say things straight and are always wrapping up the truth in jargon, politically correct speech and evasion. I'll insist until I get it out of them in plain English."

Do you need consensus?

Don't go for consensus for its own sake. Ask yourself: Can you get it? Do you need it? If the answer to both is yes, then do not underestimate its importance. As Jane Campbell said: "Consensus is a word that's got a bad name unfairly. Sometimes you need to build a consensus so as to move forward, and if you can, then you can proceed with huge strength."

But be careful that the consensus is the right thing for the organization and not about keeping people happy. If you aren't going to get it and in fact you don't really need it, but you just do not want to be out there on your own, get over it. As Michael Hastings said: "Seeking consensus, avoiding disagreement, sometimes means that pace is lost, mediocrity becomes the norm and the culture avoids decisions."

Risk: what's your attitude to it?

Risk comes in many forms and, as discussed in the earlier section about whether you can "afford" to chair (Chapter 2), being able to afford possible risks to your reputation, or indeed being sued, is part of this. Then again, Prue Leith's view was that: "Risk is a good thing, you can't always be covering your back."

Pam Chesters said sub-committees play an important role in risk management: "Sub-committees often emerge from risk assessment. You see an area of real risk which needs a level of supervision and scrutiny that the full board couldn't provide, so you create a sub-committee to do it." While

Stephen Falder was very clear that, in the end, it's all about: "Risk to reputation and to self-esteem and to ego. These must be well-balanced by the rewards that the role of chair could and should bring."

Richard Greenhalgh struck a nice balance: "I like risk, I'll do risk, but I won't seek it."

And Bill Kilgallon pointed out: "Risk is part of life, of every job and every organization, and makes it exciting and interesting. Making those judgements is the best bit of being a chair." Indeed, most chairs seemed to think that if you don't buy this, don't chair, and that part of their role was to lead the way on risk and counter the forces of hesitance.

As Imtiaz Farookhi said: "Risk? Calculate it, and take it in the context of the potential rewards." And Zenna Atkins: "It's up to chairs to save boards from becoming moribund through fear of getting things wrong. This may mean reassuring them that you'll take the rap if it goes wrong."

Geraint Talfan Davies was up for some danger too: "We have to be braver than governments! They're so hooked on compliance these days, and we need to push as far as we can. Risk is an essential part of artistic activity. You have to balance it, not be cavalier about it, but weigh it up proportionate to possible gains." But he also added with passion: "To allow for risk, to encourage risk, you must make room for failure, otherwise it is meaningless." Joanna Foster concurred: "It's a real problem in the NHS, allowing ourselves to learn from our mistakes. How can we admit mega ones while fearing that our heads will be chopped off?"

Simon Fanshawe said that when it does go pear-shaped, it's both right and okay to stand up and be counted: "A man died from negligence in our local hospital and the CEO and chair made a joint statement about mistakes. I spoke to staff there who said it was hugely valuable to them, that it shifted from a blame culture to one of openness. The chair must own failures as well as successes, learning from mistakes and not hiding from them, enabling others to follow suit and, in a crisis, making it clear what will change but also what won't."

Risk comes in different forms

The chairs recommended some actions to recognize and deal with different forms of risk.

Action 1: Ensure you understand exactly what your personal liabilities are if you're sued for negligence or things go belly up in some other way.

Generally speaking, you're pretty unlikely to be held liable if you have acted reasonably and in good faith. But ask at the outset what indemnification exists for the chair/board members, such as directors' liability insurance. And keep in mind that higher standards of understanding on specific areas, such as finance, may be expected of those from relevant professional groups. As one chair said: "If I screw up on the accounts, I may be held liable or I may not, but if an accountant screws them up, he's more likely to be held liable."

Action 2: Think it all through early on. If there is risk to your reputation, face up to it and let this guide you about whether or not to take the role.

Although your chairing role may not be in the same field as that in which you developed your professional expertise, it can nevertheless put your reputation at risk. There may be situations, for example, where you may not always have full control (political agendas or interference sprang to some minds), yet the wider world may not appreciate the limits to your power and influence. Make sure you balance the risk to your reputation with the satisfaction you get from your chairing role.

Action 3: Always address, proactively, anything that could be construed as a conflict of interest.

The Nolan rules are very clear (see http://www.archive.official-docu-ments.co.uk/document/parlment/nolan/nolan.htm) and the world is hot on them. Take the time to think carefully and laterally about all your links and connections.

Action 4: Check the organization's risk analysis.

The organization should already have a formal risk register – if it doesn't, join with your eyes open. The register should highlight the key risks which could prevent delivery of the organization's strategy and the plans in hand to manage the risk.

The process by which the register is compiled and updated is as important as managing the risks identified. You need to know: How comprehensive is it? Do risks filter from the bottom up as well as top down? There are too many registers which are undynamic, become formulaic and simply get rubber-stamped.

Lesser risks should be managed below board level, but in a process which doesn't lose them. Some detailed reviews of risk may be better delivered via board sub-committees: the board can't realistically track hundreds of risks, and it needs to manage those which have the greatest possibility of causing failure of strategy.

How to reduce risk

▶ Establish the principle of "no surprises" on your first day!

▶ Ensure a culture of openness and transparency is fostered.

▶ Make sure you're not dependent solely on the CEO as your source of information as to what is going on in the organization. Develop your own antennae and encourage fellow board members to do likewise.

▶ Ensure board papers are written succinctly and unambiguously with risks and recommendations clearly highlighted.

▶ Ensure board decisions are clearly recorded and a master set of signed papers/minutes is kept securely.

▶ Standing orders governing conduct should be adhered to and regularly reviewed, updating as required.

▶ Ensure that the board agenda-planning process captures items which are to come back to the board at a later date, as "brought forwards".

▶ Honesty is the best policy – don't be afraid to get out there early and apologize.

▶ Manage your stakeholders proactively – especially if things are going wrong. Bad news emerging via the press will not advance your cause!

Action 5 – Develop the right culture.

Watch out for words like "the safe option" and "the safe candidate". Chairs felt that what had been sold to them as "safe" in the short term often landed them in a longer-term mess. Establish a culture that recognizes that "safe" isn't always safe in the long run.

Coping with serious allegations, or the smell of them

Bill Kilgallon was very clear about what to do in the face of a serious allegation: "All organizations have procedures, know them, follow them to the letter. Get involved at the right time and according to the rules."

Some chairs also spoke of the need for informal approaches in the early stages when it's "just a smell", when instinct tells you there's a problem but no one has yet come to you about it. But once they have, as one said: "Be careful. There's no such thing as an informal chat. Once you've been told something, that's it, you know it and can't pretend you don't."

And on what to do if there's a smell, Michael Hastings said: "Trust your instinct. If it tells you not to trust an exec or that there's a problem, don't wait until the evidence is so overwhelming that you have to act. By acting too late your opportunity to put things right has been lost." Zenna Atkins agreed: "There's rarely smoke without fire, although the problem might not be what you at first thought it was. Put out your radar at the first hint of trouble and find out as much as you can unofficially. Talk to individuals and form your own opinion."

Richard Greenhalgh felt similarly: "It may sometimes be best to resolve things informally. When a problem crops up, you might be able to resolve it through discussing it carefully with those involved, perhaps bringing troubled parties together with or without a mediator." He made a similar comment about weighing up what to do about media allegations: "You need to decide, use careful judgement about whether it's best to let the story run and die or do something proactive about it." And this didn't contradict the advice in the box, "Facing up to the media" (Chapter 5), about what to do when the media are breathing down your neck: if they really are, then you have to act, fast and decisively. But if they're running a story that's just not exactly what you hoped for, you may be wise, for a while, to try ignoring it.

If and when trouble becomes official, Imtiaz Farookhi said: "You need a process, and this is as important as the result." Richard Greenhalgh added: "Treat different kinds of allegations differently. If they're to do with an employment issue, I'm a stickler for following the rules. Get the lawyers in."

Geraint Talfan Davies spoke up for ensuring that people know how to raise concerns: "You must have a whistleblowers' code in place so that staff know they can raise things at board level." But, set against this, all the chairs had experience of time wasters. As Simon Fanshawe said: "It depends who's making the allegation. Sometimes you know it's someone out to make trouble, and you can decide to ignore their allegations." Prue Leith advised greater caution: "Even if you know it's nonsense, go into procedural mode. Everything will be resolved this way. It's a bit like food poisoning cropping up in a restaurant – you call the environmental health people and get the procedure started. Doing it seriously and formally is the best defence, and if it's all fine, you'll be clearly exonerated."

There was also a warning against dismissing the trivial in case it's masking something bigger. As one chair said: "Someone tells me that Tony's stealing pencils and pens, I ask the accuser why they told me and they say 'because I thought you should know'. Then, when I ask if they want me to pursue it, they say, 'Oh well, you can't do anything.' But it alerts you as well as annoying you. It may turn out to have been the head of a boil and sometimes underneath you find an inter-organizational feud."

Finally, some miscellaneous but invaluable pieces of advice were:

▶ Get the respective roles of the CEO and chair very clear, who is dealing with which bits of which allegations.

▶ Never, ever try to cover anything up.

▶ Be generous in victory.

▶ Resign if you made the wrong call.

▶ And, as Prue said: "A crisis is when all chairs have to have devices to strengthen their backbones, and to be very clear what their own ethics are."

Trouble brewing

It shouldn't, the chairs said, unless you've got the culture wrong. If the culture's right, things won't brew but will emerge, and emerge positively. As Richard Ellis said: "I've tried to create an open culture so things really don't brew." Geraint Talfan Davies added: "People tell me if things aren't working, there's nothing under-the-counter about it."

Prue Leith said: "I don't often find myself in the middle of storms because I hate rows and I'm good at spotting them before they erupt."

So, what sort of things is she looking for, or listening to?

Michael Hastings said it's about people avoiding your questions: "Then you know they either love you too much to hurt you, or don't love you at all. Either way, you're in trouble!" While Richard Greenhalgh said: "It's poor attendance, and less rebellion than disaffection. Spot this, ask about it, and you'll avoid rebellion."

Zenna Atkins said: "It's when people avoid direct eye contact that you need to find out what's going on, and board members looking at each other, exchanging glances. It's quite amazing how people give themselves away." She added: "I know I'm naïve, but I hadn't taken in that there are people on NHS boards who are more wedded to the organization than to people's health. I could have seen it, but didn't. They fed me lines and I ate them for some time."

Further to her comment about avoiding real storms, Prue Leith said: "When someone says, 'I wonder if I can just have a word with you,' I give them the time immediately. My heart sinks of course if it's skullduggery or a resignation. But usually it's a chance to resolve a molehill before it grows into a mountain."

Early warning signs of trouble brewing

▶ Meetings overrun.

▶ People don't turn up.

▶ Decisions aren't made or are postponed.

▶ Bad temperedness.

▶ The minute the meeting ends, everyone is out.

▶ Friction between chair and CEO.

▶ Board members or executives won't take criticism.

▶ People are disparaging about the client group or stakeholders – as Prue Leith said: "Beware the word 'punters' rather than 'customers'."

▶ Internal focus.

▶ David Isaac said: "You start discussing how you support board members rather than the people you are there to serve."

▶ No one has read the papers, not even you.

▶ Body language that says disengagement or boredom.

▶ Quiet meetings.

▶ CEO asks you to sign a paper confirming something you've said.

▶ CEO brings you decisions that have to be made instantly, now, this minute.

▶ Most of the agenda items are for noting only.

▶ Long, dense, unsummarized or late papers.

▶ Soggy answers to questions.

▶ Carolyn Berkeley said: "Spot the 'Ah well' answers that seek to excuse performance. 'Ah well, with their funds or bigger premises maybe we could. . .'"

Chairing for the government

Some chairs, like Prue Leith, said they simply never would chair a government organization, : "I wouldn't do it. I've twice had my hat in the ring for such a post, and both times withdrew when I realized just how much the government department would meddle." Carolyn Berkeley said she once heard the nature of the situation explained very well to one of her new board members: "Think of it as a subsidiary board, not as the main board, and indeed a subsidiary where there's no member of the main board present, but where the nominated main board person is watching over your shoulder."

And while it may look hard to achieve, contradictory at times, and set against impossible odds, the advice from those who have made chairing for the government work was clear.

Be realistic

If you're chairing for government, you can't expect total independence. Indeed, even if you're not delivering for government but are mainly or wholly funded by it, however strong the claims of independence, if you can't cope with the lack of independence, then, like Prue Leith, don't do it.

Richard Greenhalgh said: "With public sector chairing, the government is your major or only investor, so think about how you would treat them in business. Always be sensitive to the big issues, ask advice, keep them informed, deliver policy implementation as you would deliver profit." And Stephen Falder recalled how he once got it wrong: "I did get my fingers burnt once. Out of blindness and lack of common sense, I joined because it seemed like a good idea, without questioning whether it would actually work and without facing up to the fact that we would be a government marionette not a board."

Get the brief right

Andrew Cubie, recalling his time chairing a major review of university funding in Scotland, advised: "You must identify principles before details. I had a government board of 14 people and we spent time and effort getting our underpinning principles clear, for instance that we would encourage an increase in the scope of higher education, making it more accessible to those excluded from it. From this starting point, and always keeping close to it, it was much easier to proceed and move ahead with the details."

Don't cower

Again, Andrew Cubie said: "You have to be aware that the civil service is obliged to represent a set of policies set out for them, and that you as chair have to be robust in asserting your independence." This was echoed by many. "Never toe the line because your stakeholder is government or local government. Don't shut up," said Simon Fanshawe. And from Jane Campbell: "A few years ago when I was chairing a medium-sized voluntary sector board, we were being pushed by our sponsor to take over a project and we knew that to say no would be very difficult. I saw each board member separately, had a board meeting devoted to that issue, and then went back to the sponsor and said no. It was a huge risk and if they had said I had to do it I would have had to resign rather than go against my board. At least I know I can go home and sleep at nights, lots of chairs don't."

Carolyn Berkeley said: "The real eye-opener for me was seeing that they can be taken on. There's almost a conspiracy to get you to over-respect civil servants and the government, they almost inoculate you. Make sure you don't succumb."

Get the rules of engagement clear

Imtiaz Farookhi said this is "Utterly vital," while Richard Greenhalgh added: "You need to know how much independence you have over things like deciding the chief executive's pay, what the route for appraisal is, things like that. Not being clear from the start causes aggravation."

Be smart

One time when this is particularly important is in pre-election mode. Some of the pressure the government is feeling is sure to find its way down to you, especially if your minister is in a marginal seat. Carolyn Berkeley pointed out: "Beware, in the run up, not to be persuaded to favour, in terms of your briefings, the sitting MP. You need to deal equally with the different candidates as you're delivering to the people you serve irrespective of who's in power."

Don't expect too much

Least of all consistency! Geraint Talfan Davies said: "While governments often work on the 'arm's length principle', that arm is often telescopic when those in power want it to be. This can mean that governments either distance themselves from difficult situations, which can make you feel uncomfortable, or want to be involved in running organizations which they ultimately control." And they may sway between the two within a day.

Richard Greenhalgh warned: "It gets complex if the government wants to micro-manage. They're clever people, civil servants, but they're risk averse, and it's undeniably complex for them under the glare of publicity."

And other tips for smoother chairing when government is close? The best were:

"Spend time recognizing the political realities and waves, you can ride them for the good of your organization. Or, if you need to, choose the right time and start your own wave."

Richard Ellis

"Know whose boots you have to lick if you want a second chance, and take special care over that relationship."

John Gardiner

"Be skilful. Understand the pressures they're under and work with them to achieve your aims. If you want to oppose change, understand their drive and be clever about it."

Bill Kilgallon

"Push against timidity, even when you're putting public money at risk."

Richard Ellis

And a few from those who preferred to remain nameless:

"There may be lots of things going on behind the scenes that you won't spot. For example, if the chair of a public body's board is dealing with important issues, they can be certain that there'll be a shadow of their board dealing with the same issue within government."

"Never accept statutory appointees without fixed terms of office. If they don't perform, your chances of moving them on before their term is up are minimal, so at least make sure there's a term."

"Be clear that you'll only ever get negative feedback from ministers unless you're in the reappointment phase and they want you to stay on."

How do you know who you can trust?

Most chairs said you have to start with a degree of trust. As Imtiaz Farookhi put it: "I trust people unless I have a reason not to." But within this, chairs suggested that you should always proceed with caution.

Richard Ellis said: "Look, listen and learn. This is the best way to figure out who's spinning you a line. Make the most of your virginity, in the first few months, ask silly questions that may be harder to ask later." Andrew Cubie's view was: "Clearly you will not have immediate respect for those you're involved with as a chair, but always have respect for and patience in understanding their views. Don't jump to conclusions based on people's labels, and always keep in mind that if, as often happens, you've had no hand in selecting the board, you need to take time to understand what they care about."

Simon Fanshawe said: "Chairing is a very political role. Everyone has their own agenda, motives, life view and reasons for being on the board. You'll gradually feel more secure in the role and happy to ask questions." But he also said: "You never really know someone until you've gone through something with them, that's when you discover who to trust. Boards are like tea bags, you never know how good they are until they've been in hot water!"

Prue Leith advised that you find out who to trust through "diplomacy and lots of reading," and she warned: "Certainly no confiding, especially in the early days." Though she said she's been lucky: "I've always known who to trust because I've either owned the company, come in as a chair having already been on the board or joined having already got to know the people well." While Richard Greenhalgh said that even if you have worked out the ones to look out for, those that on the whole you can't trust, you should still: "Take them aside, don't berate but flatter them, and you may find you can turn round a board member from being a member of the awkward squad to being trusted."

Peter Sherratt said you need to spot both the good and the bad: "When you're trying to figure out who to trust, look for the genuine people who totally disregard their own personal interests in trying to find the right solution for the organization. Look closely at how genuine people are when they express their opinions, whether they parrot something they've read or have thought about it and are expressing something that they genuinely feel."

Zenna Atkins picked up on Prue Leith's first point, saying: "No confiding, ever. If you want to moan, go elsewhere, however much you trust your colleagues," she also went on to put an interesting spin on the whole question of trust: "What is it that you're trusting them to do exactly? Board members should have job descriptions and be performance-managed. I don't trust people to do what they're supposed to do, I expect them to do it, and manage them if they don't. I don't care whether they're paid or not, they're there to do a role which they have agreed to. For commercial or publicly sensitive stuff, I state that if they blab, I fire them. I don't need the board members as sounding boards, confidantes or friends, I need them to serve the organization well. If I need to check things out, test ideas and so on, I can go elsewhere, or buy in expertise."

7

And finally

How do chairs look after themselves?

If the chair's role, as stated earlier in this book, is "about being isolated, vulnerable, occasionally disliked and generally thick skinned" and you need distance to cope and to enable you to see the wood from the trees, what can you do to help yourself?

Avid readers will have noted Jane Campbell's admission that the best thing she ever did was swallow her pride and ask for a mentor. While most chairs said they felt bad about spending the organization's training or consultancy budgets on themselves, they also realized that this had to happen sometimes, and many praised courses they had been on. But for almost all, learning from others had been invaluable.

Pairing up with other chairs was seen by some as especially useful if the pairing was with a chair from another sector, because this reduced possibilities for rivalry and left them to concentrate on things to do with chairing. This worked particularly well for experienced chairs who wanted to go on learning. As Michael Hastings said: "Find a chair you can learn from, and go to their meeting."

The value of having "people to ask" was also clear. As Zenna Atkins said: "You expect people to be annoyed about being asked for help or information or clarity, and fear that they will think you're floundering, but they're usually flattered."

Bill Kilgallon spoke of having a network for "mutual support from others in the same position", in his case provided through the NHS Confederation, the trade body for NHS trusts, and he added: "There are also people whose specific technical skills are invaluable at specific times, such as the hospital's medical director." And Geraint Talfan Davies said: "I know relevant specialists for specific things, but talk to my closest friend, now retired, for the rest. He's very wise. He doesn't know my sector in detail but he's just got this canny understanding." While Stephen Falder reflected: "I'm the annoying one who collects business cards when people say, 'Do call if I can ever be of help,' and then I really do call them!"

Finally, Stephen and pretty much all the others highlighted the dangers of trying to take everything on unaided and of failing to spot weaknesses or blind-spots and not therefore being able to make sure someone else covers them. As Michael Hastings said: "If you're not a financial whizz, make sure someone else on the board is." Or Zenna Atkins: "I'm not a cuddly team type, so I need some of my board members to be." Or the one who said: "If you're not the media type, get someone else, the CEO or another board member, who's good at it."

For how long should you chair?

"For as long as you have fresh energy and vision. For as long as you're useful."

Simon Fanshawe

"If you're fresh and open to new ideas and adding value, it's fine to stay."

Peter Sherratt

"If it's going badly and you're responsible, then you go."

Bill Kilgallon

And the signs that it's time to go?

"When you hear them say, 'Oh, you must stay,' what they really mean is that they're too lazy to find a successor."

Simon Fanshawe

"When you hear yourself say, 'As I've said before,' because you realize that you've really got nothing new to say."

Zenna Atkins

"When you hear 'we tried this ten years ago' too often at board meetings. Face it, you've become part of the furniture and it's time to go."

Prue Leith

"When you hear yourself groan when the papers arrive."

Prue Leith

"When you wake up on the morning of three consecutive board meetings saying, 'Oh no,' basically, you've lost the passion."

Bill Kilgallon

So, when does the time come to go?

Richard Ellis said: "I think two to three years is needed to get things going and start to get them done, so five to seven years in post is probably right." Prue Leith suggested following the "rules": "Higgs says seven years is probably ideal, 16 is certainly too long. And don't kid yourself that restructuring means you should serve seven under each structure."

Bill Kilgallon made the case for clarity: "Stay for a fixed term of three to four years with a maximum of two renewals based on performance, or, as an exception, if there's a major ongoing event with lots of liaison, you might extend your term of office till the job's done." And Stephen Falder reinforced this: "You need to know a fixed term at the outset and stick to it. That way you can focus on a job with a beginning, a middle and an end. Say no to a chair role that goes on 'until we get a new chair' and only change a fixed term if it's clearly unfeasible to do something useful in the time set, and then change the length early on and with the board's consent."

You should also leave if you get something badly wrong, as Peter Sherratt said: "If I had a real belief in one strategic direction, I'd listen to those saying no, but I'd stick my neck out and explain my reasons for going for my view. If I then found I'd made the wrong call, I'd resign as chair."

And when you do stand down as chair, as one said: "Leave it strong. Ideally go when the organization is running well, so you hand over a going concern to someone who'll bring a new dimension. It's all about Charles Handy and his sigmoid curve – change things when they're going well."

Richard Ellis said: "One thing I have always done with organizations is to try to help find my successor. With a Public Board appointments process it is clearly different, but I can still enthuse and encourage potential candidates to apply! I do think leaders have a responsibility to develop their successors."

When to go – a personal view

If you can't sleep at night because you're doing it, then say no, or stop. I knew I needed to be above reproach as chair of Forum for the Future and when I realized I was scared there'd be a piece in the press about how I didn't have a solar-panelled house or an organic garden, then it was time to go.

Prue Leith, on her decision to stand down as chair

It's certainly time to go when:

▶ you're no longer excited by the organization and, more importantly, by those it serves;

▶ you've made ten identical speeches on the organization's behalf;

▶ you and the chief executive think so alike you no longer challenge each other;

▶ you skip through all the papers because you know them all;

▶ you know the organization needs change but you haven't got the time/stomach/energy for it;

▶ the key stakeholders aren't excited about seeing you;

▶ your board members are doing it by rote;

▶ you feel tired, jaded or that you've run out of courage on certain issues;

- you're no longer learning in the role;

- you've become so passionate about the place that you've become blinded; your passion must drive you, but cannot blind you.

Looking back, what makes you laugh or shudder?

Imtiaz Farookhi said: "Turning up at a meeting not having read the papers. I do it too often and usually get away with it, but the thought causes a small shudder."

For Michael Hastings, it was: "All the times I've gone with the flow and not stood up and trusted my own judgement and then been left to clear up the mess with no one to blame!"

Zenna Atkins laughed about the time when: "There was a private meeting which overran before a full board meeting in public, so I had to spend 45 minutes entertaining the public. I loved it! I laugh with hindsight, but I was shitting a brick beforehand." And she shuddered about: "The media stuff – it can be so volatile and so sensitive."

Richard Ellis remembered letting a man who he found hugely irritating wind him up, until: "In the end I actually lost it, lost my rag publicly. It was a disaster." While Prue Leith shuddered at memories of sacking chief executives: "Especially when they are good people in the wrong job at the wrong time."

She also remembered a time when she got it totally wrong, laughed something off without realizing or thinking how important it was to her audience: "As the new chair of the Royal Society of Arts I decided, given the average age (62) and sex (mostly male) of the membership then, to call myself chairman rather than chair. Early on I held a big meeting because we needed to attract more women. When the highly able, serious and feminist audience asked me why I continued to refer to myself as chairman, I gave a flippant and would-be funny response. Of course, however much I apologized and admitted that language was fundamental to attitude and change, the damage was done: I had managed to alienate a sector of society I really wanted to woo – we needed them in the RSA. But there were no more of those meetings. I've never forgotten that one!"

Bill Kilgallon laughed – looking back – about making a fool of himself: "The night I went unprepared into a meeting of hostile senior medical staff. I should have known this through my own efforts – reading and asking around – and through being better advised. I was too confident. Sometimes you can busk, but not with experts."

Simon Fanshawe spoke of two occasions of downfall which make him giggle now:

"Forgetting people's names is awful, and worst when you're confident, certain. You say, 'Julia. . .,' and they say, 'It's Jo. . .' Always know the names of all your board members, but if you really can't, if you're hopeless at it, don't use names, or have name cards." And then, even worse, he recalled: "It's so easy to go with gusto – with confidence – and say, 'It's really complex and we must work hard together to find out. . .,' and someone looks up and says, 'Err, the answer's three,' and everyone else knew. You look pretty stupid."

But he also cautioned, as did most other chairs, that it's better to ask if you don't know something, even at risk of looking stupid, than pretend it's clear. Though he did add that if you're really worried that your stupidity over one particular thing is monumental, then: "Okay, sometimes it's best to ask your brother-in-law in private."

A pretty common message from these stories is that while they may be mostly about laughing now, they were about shuddering back then. And maybe that's the truth of chairing, that it makes your life more interesting, even more fun, helps other people through its achievements, but is not done easily. And it takes time, as Stephen Falder said: "It makes me laugh to think of all those times when I fell for the line, 'It's only a couple of meetings a year!'"

And finally, laugh or shudder?

The thing never to do as a chair? That's easy – I know, because I've done it. Never, ever take your jacket off at the beginning of a large public board meeting forgetting you only have a bra underneath.

Zenna Atkins